Conversation
Inspirations

Over Two Thousand
Conversation Topics
Second, Revised Edition

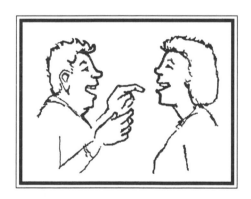

Nancy Ellen Zelman, Esq.

Illustrated by Patrick R. Moran

Supplementary Materials Handbook Three

PRO LINGUA ASSOCIATES

Brattleboro, Vermont

Pro Lingus Associates, Publishers
P.O. Box 1348
Brattleboro, VT 05302 USA
Office 802-257-7779
Orders 800-366-4775
San 216-0576

At Pro Lingua,
our objective is to foster an approach
to learning and teaching that we call
***interplay**, the **inter**action of language*
learners and teachers with their materials,
with the language and culture,
and with each other in active, creative,
*and productive **play**.*

This book was designed and set by Arthur A. Burrows using Old Style Bookman text and display type. It was printed and bound by BookCrafters of Fredericksburg, Virginia.

Printed in the United States of America

Second edition. Third printing 2000
19,000 copies in print

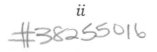

Contents

Introduction

The primary focus of this book is to promote conversational fluency for students studying English. However, **Conversation Inspirations** can be used in many other situations where the primary focus is on facilitating language acquisition or understanding modern American culture. It may also be adapted for teaching other languages; this can raise interesting cultural issues – you should think about these before assigning a topic.

You will also find that these topics easily lend themselves to writing assignments. After role plays, for example, you can have your students write a dialogue. When using discussion topics, you can have students write essays. The possibilities are endless.

Grouped into five kinds of conversational activities, **Conversation Inspirations** is a collection of almost 2,200 topics. For each activity there is a description of suggested procedures for the teacher.

A very effective way of using the topics listed in this book is to write the topic on a 3 X 5 index card and give the card to the students to hold and refer to as they engage in the activity. This very simple device not only creates the effect of playing a kind of card game, it also allows the teacher to build a collection of cards that can be used over and over. The cards can be retained after each activity and stored in a small file box for future use.

Although you may choose to use and store these cards in different ways, their day-to-day use can be facilitated by following the simple classification system presented in the book. The book then becomes a quick and easy index to what is contained in the file box. Each section is coded according to the name of the activity, and the topical area. Thus **R-ad** means role play (activity) advice (topic area). The code is given after each topic – see page x for further explanation of the code system.

The number of topics presented in this book is finite, but it is obvious that the potential list is endless. Many of the topics can be modified by switching the characters. For example, "Ask your roommate" can be changed to "Ask your friend" or "Ask your child." The gender pronouns are also interchangeable. In the text, there are as many masculine pronouns as feminine in an attempt to evenly distribute the topics. Most topics can be adapted to fit either gender. Additionally, topics listed under one activity, such as "Interviews", may be used in another kind of activities, for example, in "Discussions". You are limited only by your ingenuity.

These topics can be used in a variety of ways, from totally free conversation to carefully monitored conversation. The general procedure and mistake correction techniques outlined in the next few pages will help your students increase their cultural awareness and social skills as well as the accuracy of their spoken English.

Monitored Conversation Procedure

This basic procedure can be used with most of the activities and with students with intermediate language skills:

1. Call two students up to the front of the class and ask them to sit in two chairs facing each other, while the rest of the class is seated in a semi-circle. The students seated in the "hot seats" get a conversation card.

2. Explain that the two students up front must speak to each other for three minutes, talking about the situation or topic on the card.

3. Explain that the cards merely function to promote linguistic interaction, and that what is important is not the topic *per se*, but the language used by the two students.

4. Then explain the responsibility of the monitoring students, which is to listen to the students in the hot seats for inappropriate speech, mispronunciation, and incorrect grammar. When a mistake is heard, the listeners write down (as best they can) the phrase or sentence in which the mistake was made. The listener's job is to practice responsible listening. Explain that this is just as important as the speakers' jobs because an awareness of mistakes is the first step toward avoiding the same mistakes in one's own speech.

5. As an alternative, assign half the class to listen to one of the speakers, and rest of the class to the other.

6. One of the listeners gets the job of timekeeper. When the pair in front is ready and has decided on who plays which part in the role play, the timekeeper says "Go" and the speakers converse.

7. At the end of three minutes, the timekeeper says, "Stop."

8. Call upon the listeners one at a time to identify the mistakes that they have heard.

9. The student who has made the mistake tries to correct it, but if unable to do so, the other listeners can be called upon to make the correction.

10. If no one is able to correct the mistake, the teacher may then explain the problem. The teacher can then ask all the students to write the mistake in their notebooks and next to it a large "X". Then correct the mistake and have all the students write the correct form in their books.

Note: A few of the role plays require more than two people to participate in the "hot seats". The procedure detailed above can easily be modified to accommodate three speakers.

For beginning students or those with very limited proficiency, appropriate vocabulary and phrases should be introduced first. The teacher can also write sample sentences on the board, and point to them during the conversation. The students in the "hot seats" can then read the sentences from the board. If necessary, the teacher or two additional students can sit behind the speakers and act as "prompters." The prompters can feed the speakers lines that would be appropriate for the topic. A one-minute conversation is probably sufficient at this level.

Encourage the students who are not speaking to listen carefully for mistakes. You may wish to have the listening students focus only on one specific type of error, such as pronunciation. You can also have half the class listen for grammatical errors, for example, while the rest of the class listens to the speakers' pronunciation.

Although the skills of listening for mistakes and writing them down immediately is very difficult at this beginning level, all students can develop this skill with time and practice.

Mistake/Correction Cards

At the first conversation class, hand out blank index cards and have the students write their names at the top. Tell the students to bring these cards with them each time they have conversation class. These cards can be called mistake cards, correction cards, or whatever you and your students decide. On these cards the teacher will write the errors that the students make when they are engaged in a conversation activity. Point out to the students that this is a rare opportunity for you to help each of them individually with their own language problems.

When two students are called up to the "hot seats" they give you their mistake cards. As the listeners are writing (in their notebooks) the errors they hear, you are writing the mistakes on the participants' mistake cards. When the three-minute conversation is completed, and you have gone around the room asking the listeners to identify the problems, read the additional errors you have that none of the monitoring students identified.

Note: It is important to be aware that not every mistake must be corrected at this time. Usually five mistakes in addition to those the students have found will be quite sufficient. The students who make these mistakes should always be encouraged, not discouraged.

Call on the students to make the corrections, and have the other students repeat the correct form and copy it into their notebooks. When this is completed, return the mistake cards to their owners. The cards will only have the mistakes written on them, so inform the students that it is their responsibility to correct these cards (preferably written in a different ink color or pencil so the corrections can be seen) and to study them. Since the class has just gone over the mistakes orally, the students should immediately correct the card and study the correct forms.

Once a week you can collect all the students' mistake cards and give them an oral quiz by calling on each student and reading out loud one of the mistakes on that student's card. You may want to call on other students in the class to see if they are able to correct the mistakes that their classmates have made.

Another activity which can be used with mistake cards involves collecting all cards and dictating to the students the incorrect forms that were used by the students. Be sure the class is aware that these are not the correct forms. (You may want them to write the incorrect forms with a big "X" through them.) Then have the students work on finding the mistakes and making the corrections. At the end of class, dictate the corrected sentences for the students.

Alternatively, you can prepare a mistake sheet from incorrect sentences on the mistake cards. The students can then work from the paper in groups or individually, correcting the mistakes that they find.

Mistake Correction

It is very important that the students themselves try to recognize their own mistakes. If they are able to do this, they are at least aware of the correct form, and with more practice, they will become more accurate in their speech. Your job is to facilitate the students' realization of these errors by simply calling attention to the fact that an error has been made. You should be the last person to correct the mistakes, not the first. All the students in the class should work on trying to figure out the correction, and only after this has failed should you intervene. In this way, each student has the responsibility for thinking about linguistic accuracy.

It is not easy for students to hear their own mispronunciation, but they can discern the pronunciation of others. If and when the listening students hear something that they do not understand or they know is not pronounced accurately, have them jot the word or the phrase in quotation marks. In this way the students will know which errors in their notes were pronunciation errors. You may want to have all the students repeat the correct pronunciations after you have gone over the grammatical errors.

You may also find it helpful to use the corrections as a springboard for a mini grammar or pronunciation lesson, using substitution drills. For example:

Student A: *I don't know tennis.*

Teacher: *Can anyone correct this sentence?*

Student B: *I don't know how to play tennis.*

Teacher: *Good! Basketball...*

Student A: *I don't know how to play basketball.*

or

Student A: *They "leave" in the country.*

Teacher: *Can anyone improve the pronunciation in this sentence?*

Student B: *They live in the country.*

Teacher: *Good! In the city...*

Student A: *They live in the city.*

Teacher: *Which is correct, #1 or #2? #1 is "leave", #2 is "live". Leave.*

Student A: *Number one.*

Teacher: *Live.*

Student A: *Number two.*

In this way you are including all the students in the correction process, and not only the student who has made the original mistake.

After the students have been in the "hot seat" and their mistake cards have been returned, allow sufficient time for them to look over their cards and to correct the mistakes. If the students wait too long, they may forget the explanation and correction.

All error correction is done solely for the benefit of the students, and it is important for you to be aware that some students (especially at first) may be intimidated by this correction procedure. It is up to you to do this error correction gently, with teaching as the aim, not fault finding. At the beginning, one or two errors corrected may be sufficient for each student, and as the students become more comfortable with the procedure, the amount of error correction may be increased.

Mistake Card Fun

Game #1 Make a list of the students in the class on the blackboard. Collect the students' mistake cards. Read off one or two mistakes from each card. If a student thinks the mistake is his, he must raise a hand. If he is correct and the mistake was something he said, the student tries to correct himself. If he is unable to correct the mistake, the first person in the class to raise his hand gets the opportunity to correct it and get or lose a point. If no one is able to correct the mistake, the teacher should once again correct the mistake at the blackboard and have all the students copy the corrected form. At the end of the allotted time, the student with the most points is the winner.

Game #2 Collect all the mistake cards, and at home, make up a list of incorrect sentences. Then divide the class into two or three groups, and give each group a copy of the incorrect sentences. The first group to correct the most sentences wins. A variation of this can be to make a list of correct and incorrect sentences, and have the students identify the correct sentences and correct the incorrect ones.

Game #3   From the mistake cards, dictate a sentence with an error in it. The first student to correct the sentence wins a point.

How to Prepare Your Topic Cards

Take a standard, unlined 3 x 5 index card. Either copy the selected topic onto the card, or photocopy the topic and paste it to the card using a glue stick. In either case, some teachers find it is helpful to have their students help prepare the cards

To help you keep the various activities and topics together in your card file, you may find it useful to copy in large letters at the top right hand corner of each card the small code that appears after the topic. On the sample below, the code **R-ad** means "Role Play: Advice." The activities can be color coded as well by using blue cards for role-play topics, yellow for interviews, pink for talks, etc.

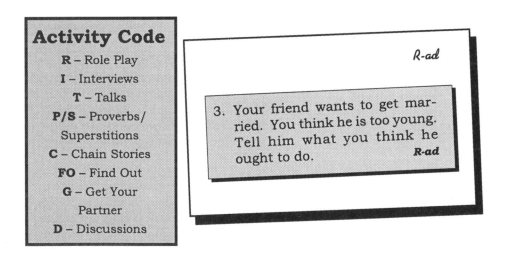

Activity Code

R – Role Play
I – Interviews
T – Talks
P/S – Proverbs/ Superstitions
C – Chain Stories
FO – Find Out
G – Get Your Partner
D – Discussions

R-ad

3. Your friend wants to get married. You think he is too young. Tell him what you think he ought to do.   **R-ad**

Index cards are inexpensive and will last through many uses, but some teachers like to laminate their completed cards. This does protect them and makes them last longer. And it may encourage some students to treat both the cards and the activity with more respect.

Conversation Inspirations

To my mother and father
to Josh and Kory
and to those who love me

With thanks for your inspirations

ROLE PLAYS

Role plays require the students to assume an identity and think and speak in that character's identity. For some students this is much easier than expressing themselves personally.

Procedures for Role Plays

With minor variations, procedures for Role Plays can be used with any other topic presented in this book.

#1. Have two students come to the front of the classroom and take the "hot seats." Give (or have the students choose) a role playing card, and have them follow the monitored conversation procedure as described in the introduction.

#2. Divide the class into small groups of 3-5 students and give each group a role playing card. Two students must engage in conversation and the other students are assigned to monitor the students who are speaking. After three minutes, the groups go over the mistakes they noticed while you circulate and answer questions, aiding and correcting. You may want to ask the students who are speaking to put their mistake cards on the desk in front of them. Then, as the students engage in the activity, you can circulate, sitting in on each group and writing the mistakes you hear on the mistake cards. After the students go over the mistakes they have found, the students read their mistake cards out loud and the entire group works on correction.

#3. Group the students in pairs and ask all the students to turn their mistake cards upside down, so they will face you as you walk around the room. Give each pair a role playing card and ask each pair to begin talking about the card. During this time, circulate, listen in on each pair, and write one or two mistakes on their corresponding mistake cards. At the end of three minutes, instruct the pairs to pass their role playing cards to the left.

This procedure of timing the conversations, noting the mistakes on mistake cards, and passing cards to the next pair is repeated until each pair has seen each role playing card. Then the students can look at their mistake cards and together with their partners, correct the mistakes that were made. You can assist in this, working with each pair.

#4. Divide the students into pairs and give each set the same (or different) role playing cards. The students have fifteen minutes to prepare a short role play to the class. You can monitor the mistakes using the monitored conversation procedure.

#5. Group the students into pairs and ask them to write a dialogue that will be presented to the class. You can use monitored conversation procedure to monitor, or you can collect the dialogues and correct them.

#6. You may want to introduce selected new vocabulary before a role play or dialogue. The students can be asked to use these words in their conversation. This can be made into a game where the pair using the most new vocabulary correctly in their role play is the winner.

Advice

1. Your friend is getting very drunk at a party. Tell her not to drink so much. *R-ad*

2. Your friend was just fired from his job because of rudeness to his employer. Tell him what you think he should do. *R-ad*

3. Your friend wants to get married. You think he is too young. Tell him what you think he ought to do. *R-ad*

4. Your friend thinks that she is pregnant, and she comes to you for advice. What should she do? *R-ad*

5. Your friend's girlfriend is pregnant. Your friend comes to you to find out what you think he should do. *R-ad*

6. You saw your neighbor slap his little child. Ask your friend what she thinks you should do about it. *R-ad*

7. Your friend looks very tired, and you know your friend could use some rest. Convince your friend to take it easy. *R-ad*

8. Your friend is thinking about running for City Council. You don't think your friend is qualified for the position. Tell your friend that you are certain it will cost a lot of money and you don't think it is a good idea. *R-ad*

9. You are studying at a very prestigious school. Your best friend would like to transfer to your school. Advise your friend on what to do to get accepted. *R-ad*

10. Your house is infested with fleas. Call the landlady and ask her what to do. *R-ad*

11. It is very difficult for you to pay your bills. Ask your friend which he thinks you should do, drop out of school and get a job or stay in school with very little money. *R-ad*

12. Your friend is having problems with his teenage child. Tell your friend what you would do in his situation. *R-ad*

13. You bought a new car several months ago, but now find that you are unable to make the payments. Talk to the car dealer and explain your problem. *R-ad*

14. You are taking a trip to Europe tomorrow. You knew you had your passport, but you just can't seem to find it. Ask your travel agent what you can do. *R-ad*

15. Two of your best friends just had a tremendous fight. Go over to the house of one of them and convince him to apologize. *R-ad*

16. You think your best friend's wife is coming on to you sexually. Talk to another friend about what you should do. *R-ad*

17. Although you have a boyfriend, you just met someone new who is very attractive to you. Ask your friend for advice on what to do. *R-ad*

18. You found out your friend is using illegal drugs. Tell him how you feel about this and give him your advice. *R-ad*

19. You are so worried about final exams that you are physically ill. Talk to your parent about your problem.   *R-ad*

20. You parked your car in an illegal parking spot. You come out of a shop and find that it is being towed away. Find out from the policeman what you should do.   *R-ad*

21. Your house is next to the airport and the noise is driving you crazy. Ask your friend what you should do.   *R-ad*

22. Every time you go anywhere you get lost. Ask your friend what you can do.   *R-ad*

23. Your friends want to fly to the Caribbean for a vacation. You have never told anyone but you are terribly afraid of flying. Talk to your friends about your problem.   *R-ad*

24. Your friend is gay, but she has not told her parents. Next weekend you and your friend are going to be at her parents' home for a family get-together and she is thinking about telling them at that time. Tell your friend how you feel about her timing.   *R-ad*

25. Your friend has been gaining a lot of weight. Tell him what he should do about it.   *R-ad*

26. You suspect that your partner may be cheating on you, but you are not certain. Ask a friend what you should do.   *R-ad*

27. Your friend wants to return to her native country because she misses her friends. Tell her what you think about that.   *R-ad*

28. Your roommate left for the weekend and was planning to be back Monday morning for work. It is now Tuesday night, and you are beginning to worry. Ask a friend what you should do.   *R-ad*

29. You are at a party and ready to go home. It's late at night and you can't find your keys. Tell the host of the party about your problem.   *R-ad*

30. By mistake, you made plans for the evening with two friends, both of whom you like. They do not, however, get along with each other. Ask another friend what you can do to remedy this problem.   *R-ad*

31. You have an urgent report that needs to be completed by tomorrow morning. Unfortunately, a good friend is leaving the country and tonight is the going-away party. Talk to this friend about what you can do.   *R-ad*

32. Your friend is always in need of money. For the third time this week he is asking to borrow some money from you. Tell your friend what he needs to do to get his financial problems under control.   *R-ad*

33. You see someone going into a neighbor's window. Ask your roommate what you should do. Should you call the police? *R-ad*

34. Your friend is having trouble making new friends. Tell her what she should do.   *R-ad*

35. Talk to a friend about what you ought to do to help your aging parents.   *R-ad*

36. Your friend is worried that she might have gotten AIDS from a night of unprotected sex with a new partner. Talk to her about taking an AIDS test. *R-ad*

37. You have a friend who has unprotected sex. Advise your friend to use condoms. *R-ad*

38. Your friend is considering losing his virginity. Discuss this with him. *R-ad*

39. Your friend is only 15 years old but wants to quit school and have a baby. Give her your opinion. *R-ad*

40. Your friend's parents are getting divorced. Her parents have asked her if she would prefer to live with her mom or her dad. She doesn't know what to say and comes to you for advice. *R-ad*

41. A man is standing in the street with a sign that says "Work for Food". Talk to him about what he should do. *R-ad*

42. Your friend comes to you crying. She tells you she fell down some stairs. You believe her husband has hit her. Talk to her. *R-ad*

43. Your sibling is married but is constantly fighting with his spouse. Advise him to seek marriage counseling. *R-ad*

44. Your mom recently got divorced from your dad. She hasn't dated in twenty years. She asks you for your advice on how to find a date. *R-ad*

45. You have just received your driver's license. Talk to your friend about whether to fill out the organ donor card. *R-ad*

46. Your friend tells you she is going to have triplets. She is worried that she does not have the finances to bring up three babies. Advise her on how she can bring up three babies on a limited budget. *R-ad*

47. The doctor has told your friend to stay in bed. When you arrive at your friend's house, you find he is not paying attention to what the doctor said. Talk to your friend. *R-ad*

48. Your friend is planning to marry an American in order to get citizenship. She does not love him, although the American loves her. Talk to her about this plan. *R-ad*

49. Your friend is in this country illegally. He is having trouble finding work. Give him some advice. *R-ad*

50. Your friend insists on speaking her native language and refuses to try to speak English. Talk to her. *R-ad*

51. Recently your sibling has been hanging around with a group of people who seem rather odd. Talk to your sibling about your concerns. *R-ad*

52. Your friend is carrying a gun to school. Talk to him about your fears for his safety. *R-ad*

53. Although you know it's dangerous, you are thinking about trying some illegal drugs. Confide in a friend. *R-ad*

54. A friend tells you that he knows someone is saying bad things about him behind his back. Tell your friend what he should do. *R-ad*

55. In the morning, your friend often comes to school drunk. Talk to him about getting some help for his problem.   *R-ad*

56. You go into the school bathroom after lunch and hear a friend vomiting. She tells you that this is how she is losing weight. Tell her what you think she should do.   *R-ad*

57. A friend confides in you that her father has been touching her sexually. Give her some advice on what she can do about this.   *R-ad*

58. The parents of a friend of yours are constantly drinking. Your friend feels powerless to help them. Talk to your friend about what can be done to improve the situation.   *R-ad*

59. You hear someone spreading rumors about someone you know. Tell this person how you feel about what he is doing. *R-ad*

60. You are interested in purchasing a home. Your real estate agent has shown you a house which is extraordinary, but a little out of your price range. Ask the agent what you should do.   *R-ad*

61. Someone is selling steroids at the gym. You are planning to be in a marathon and are thinking about buying steroids to help increase your performance. Talk to a friend about this.   *R-ad*

62. Your friend has just come out of a drug rehabilitation center. He asks you if he can use you as a personal reference on an application for an apartment. You do not want to hurt your friend's feelings, but you really are not sure he is responsible enough to always pay his rent. Talk to another friend about what you should do.   *R-ad*

63. Your friend is very sensitive and becomes very upset when people joke about her. Tell her how she needs to act.   *R-ad*

64. Your neighbors hired an unlicensed carpenter to work on an addition to their house. The carpenter asked the neighbors for $800 for materials and promised to return the next day. After three weeks of begging the carpenter to do the work, your neighbors realize that the carpenter was a con man. Advise your neighbor on what to do.   *R-ad*

Complaints

1. You bought an item that was marked "Final Sale." When you brought the item home, you found it did not work. Bring it back to the store.   *R–cm*

2. Complain to the store manager of a new store that the salespeople were rude to you.   *R–cm*

3. You are at a barbecue. The hamburger you were given is a little too rare for you. Ask the cook to put it back on the grill.   *R–cm*

4. Complain to the manager of your apartment building that there is too much noise at night and you can't sleep.   *R–cm*

5. You just bought a used TV at the Swap Meet. Before you leave to go home, you find an outlet and plug it in. The TV doesn't work. Go back to the person you bought it from.   *R–cm*

6. You buy a gold chain from a very expensive shop. After wearing it for several months, it turns your neck green. Bring it back to the store.   *R–cm*

7. Your neighbors are having a big party. It is two o'clock in the morning. Go next door and complain about the noise.   *R–cm*

8. Someone is smoking in the back of the bus. Complain to the driver.   *R–cm*

9. You brought your VCR into a shop to be repaired. After two weeks you are informed that it is repaired. When you take it home you find out it is still not working properly. Bring it back to the repair shop.   *R–cm*

10. You are at a movie theater watching a movie. A woman in your row is holding a screaming baby. Ask her to leave the theater so that you can enjoy the movie.   *R–cm*

11. You have just bought some groceries at the supermarket. When you look at your change you realize you have overpaid. Tell the cashier.   *R–cm*

12. You are at a concert and the quality of the sound is very poor. Complain about it.   *R–cm*

13. You are in a movie theater and the person in front of you is wearing a very large hat. Ask the person to take it off.   *R–cm*

14. You bought an article of clothing. You washed it once and it has shrunk. Bring it back to the shop.   *R–cm*

15. You bought a new car but you have had several problems with it. Tell the dealer you want your money back.   *R–cm*

16. You are waiting for a parking spot when someone who hasn't seen you takes it. Get that person to move and give you the space.   *R–cm*

17. You are at a gas station and you need to use the rest room. When you go in, you find that it is filthy and that there are no paper supplies. Complain to the station attendant.   *R–cm*

18. You just received your telephone bill. There are several calls listed that were made to a country that you have never heard of. Bring your bill into the telephone company and tell them.   *R–cm*

19. You buy some milk at the grocery store. When you get home you find that the milk is sour. Bring it right back to the supermarket.   *R–cm*

20. You bought a pair of shoes at a department store. You cut the string tying the pair together in order to see if they fit comfortably. When you try to return the shoes to the store, the salespeople will not take them because the string has been cut. Discuss this with the manager of the store.   *R–cm*

21. Your next door neighbor is always sun bathing in the nude. You can see him from your yard. Complain to him about this.   *R–cm*

22. You are paying for your child to take swimming lessons. When you arrive at the pool, you see the lifeguard has her back to the pool. Complain to the swimming instructor and insist on appropriate supervision.   *R–cm*

23. Your neighbor has a very noisy dog. It barks day and night whenever she lets it out into the backyard. Complain to her about this.   *R–cm*

24. The person sitting next to you in the library has a cold and is constantly coughing and sneezing. The library is very crowded. Tell the librarian to ask the person to leave.   *R–cm*

25. Your friend is always complaining to you about something. It's always one thing or another. Tell him that you have enough problems of your own and do not want to hear his complaints any more.   *R–cm*

26. A friend of yours is always upset and is calling you up late at night. Ask her to stop.   *R–cm*

27. Your friend always embarrasses you when you go to a restaurant because your friend talks much too loudly. Talk to your friend about this.   *R–cm*

28. Your neighbors are always leaving a lot of garbage in the street near your house. Complain about this.   *R–cm*

29. You left your children with a baby sitter. When you returned home you found the baby sitter asleep and your children crying. Talk to your baby sitter about this.   *R–cm*

30. You ordered something from a mail order catalogue. When you received the item you found that it did not fit the description of the item in the catalogue. Go to the Better Business Bureau and complain.   *R–cm*

31. You are at the airport. When your bags come off the ramp at the baggage claim, they are badly damaged. Go to the baggage office and ask for a claim form so that you can get your bags repaired free of charge.   *R–cm*

32. You have fleas in your apartment. Ask the apartment manager to get you an exterminator. You feel that the manager should pay for this service.   *R–cm*

33. Your landlord just called and told you he is raising the rent again, the third time in six months. Talk to your landlord about this.   *R–cm*

34. You have just moved into your house and find that there are several broken windows. Tell your landlady about this.   *R–cm*

35. You just bought an item of clothing at one store, and now you have gone up the street and you see it on sale for much less money at another shop. Return the item you bought to the higher priced store.   *R–cm*

36. You are in a store that you frequent often. All of a sudden, something from a top shelf falls and hits you on the shoulder. The store clerks are not busy, but they ignore what happened and don't offer you any assistance. Demand to speak to the manager.   *R–cm*

Conflict

1. Your "friend" has been talking about you behind your back. Confront him about this.   *R-cn*

2. It's two o'clock in the morning. Your friend calls you up because she is very upset.   *R-cn*

3. Your friend wants to borrow something of yours. You don't want to lend it.   *R-cn*

4. Your friend was supposed to pick you up two hours ago. He has just shown up. Tell him how angry you are.   *R-cn*

5. You want to get to sleep early. It is 10 p.m. on Sunday and a friend of yours comes over and begs you to go to a movie with her.   *R-cn*

6. There is a big dance tonight and you must take a partner with you. Ask your friend if you can borrow his girlfriend.   *R-cn*

7. You are stopped by a police officer because you are driving drunk.   *R-cn*

8. Someone is knocking at your door. It is four o'clock in the morning. Tell him to go away and let you sleep.   *R-cn*

9. Your mother is having a difficult time living alone and taking care of herself. You're worried. Talk to her about moving into a retirement home.   *R-cn*

10. You and your friend are supposed to be doing a project together. You have done a lot of work, but your friend has done nothing. Tell your friend how you feel.   *R-cn*

11. You want to watch a movie on TV but your friend wants to watch a sports match.   *R-cn*

12. You and your friend are driving to work and you see an accident. You want to stop and see if you can help, but your friend doesn't want to be late to work.   *R-cn*

13. You are driving your friend somewhere. When you ask her to put on the seat belt, she refuses.   *R-cn*

14. Someone is smoking on an elevator. Ask him to put the cigarette out.   *R-cn*

15. You are sitting in a movie theater. The people behind you are making a lot of noise. Ask them to be quiet.   *R-cn*

16. Your friend is rude to everyone but she thinks she is being funny. Tell her that you think that kind of behavior is inappropriate.   *R-cn*

17. Your friend has started to sell drugs in order to have some extra cash. Tell him that you are going to inform his parents. *R-cn*

18. Your friend is getting married soon. You have heard a lot of bad things about her fiancé. Tell your friend what you've heard.   *R-cn*

19. You see someone who you think is a friend of yours at a party. When you rush over to her, you realize that she is not your friend, but rather it is someone you had an argument with earlier in the day.   *R-cn*

20. You are leaving a supermarket and look at your receipt. You think the cashier has over-charged you. Bring this to his attention. *R-cn*

21. Your friend is always bossing you around. Tell him that you want to make your own deci-sions. *R-cn*

22. Everyone is going to a party where there are going to be drugs and alcohol. Tell your friend that you really don't want to go. *R-cn*

23. Your friend never wants to go anywhere. There's going to be a great party tomorrow night at a mutual friend's house. Convince her to go. *R-cn*

24. Your friend is laughing at some-one who is physically handi-capped. Tell him you find that kind of behavior unacceptable. *R-cn*

25. Your friend is getting drunk at a party. Tell her that it is time to go home. *R-cn*

26. Your friend is drunk but wants to drive home from the bar. Take his car keys. *R-cn*

27. Tell your parents that you are moving out of their house and getting your own place. *R-cn*

28. Tell your father that you do not want to work with him repair-ing your house anymore be-cause he gets so angry when you make mistakes. *R-cn*

29. Tell your friend that you feel he's changed and you have decided not to be his friend anymore. *R-cn*

30. Tell your friend that you wrecked her car. *R-cn*

31. Your friend wants to borrow $1,000. When you tell her you do not feel comfortable lending her so much money, she gets angry with you. *R-cn*

32. Your friend asked you to pick something up for him at the store. When you bring it home, he tells you it is not what he wanted. Your friend wants you to go back to the store and re-turn it, but you don't want to go. Tell him what you feel. *R-cn*

33. You leave your car illegally parked and go into a shop. When you come out, a police-man is writing you a ticket. Talk to him. *R-cn*

34. A relative has been visiting you. You feel that it is time this rela-tive left. Tell her. *R-cn*

35. You left your keys inside your locker at the gym. You see the janitor of the building, but she is in a rush. Ask the janitor to open your locker for you. *R-cn*

36. You are shopping in your neigh-borhood supermarket. A guard comes up to you and tells you that you are being arrested for shoplifting. Tell him you have done nothing wrong. *R-cn*

37. You paid a handyperson to make some repairs in your home. Af-ter the person has finished, you notice that the workmanship is very sloppy. Talk to her about this. *R-cn*

38. Although your landscaper told you it would cost no more than $1,000 to landscape your yard, he hands you a bill for $1,500. Tell the landscaper that you didn't agree to that price. *R-cn*

39. You bought a camera. You used it only one day and it fails to work. It has a warranty and you have the receipt. Talk to the store manager.   *R-cn*

40. You paid a TV repair shop to fix your television, but they did not fix it. Now they refuse to give your money back. Discuss this problem with your friend who is president of the Better Business Bureau.   *R-cn*

41. You bought a used car from a car dealer who promised you that the car was in fine working order. After driving around for a week, you find there is an oil leak. Bring it back to the dealer.   *R-cn*

42. You brought your car to a mechanic because you heard a funny noise from your engine. After you pay the mechanic and as you are driving your car home, you realize that the noise is still there. Go back to the mechanic.   *R-cn*

43. You want to sell your used bicycle for as much money as you can. It is only one year old, and it's in good shape. You need the money for school. Discuss the price with a friend who wants to pay as little as possible.   *R-cn*

44. You had licensed roofers put a new roof on your house; they guaranteed it would be leak-proof for five years. After the first big storm, the roof leaked. You have been calling and calling, but the roofers never return your calls. The same roofers are now putting a roof on your neighbor's house. Talk to them.   *R-cn*

45. You want to buy a new car but you don't have a lot of money to spend. The car dealer keeps showing you automobiles which are out of your price range. Talk to the dealer about what you can afford.   *R-cn*

46. You and your friend have been planning a vacation for months. After you buy your ticket and make all the arrangements, your friend changes his mind and decides not to go.   *R-cn*

47. Your friend is visiting you at your new home and you want to show her the house. Unfortunately, your new carpeting is white and your friend has muddy shoes. Ask her to take off her shoes at the door and go barefoot.   *R-cn*

48. When you unexpectedly visited your child's day care facility, you could not believe how many children were crying and how few care givers were present. Then you noticed that the facility was filthy. Demand to speak to the daycare center owner.   *R-cn*

49. After your babysitter leaves, you notice that there are several red areas on your child's body. When you ask the child what happened, you are told, "The babysitter made me promise not to tell." Go to the babysitter and find out what happened.   *R-cn*

50. Your child was in a fight at school with another child. Your daughter said the other girl was bullying her. The mother of the other girl comes to your door and says your child is the bully. Talk to the mother.   *R-cn*

Cultural Misunderstandings

1. You are here for the summer studying English and living with a host family. You do not understand English very well. You hear your host family talking about someone they don't like, and you are afraid they are talking about you. Talk to your host family about this. *R–cu*

2. You are visiting this country for the first time and you are shy and uncomfortable around Americans. An American student stops you while you are walking to class and asks you where the gymnasium is. You do not know and are embarrassed to speak. What do you say? *R–cu*

3. You are from a culture where married women wear a dot in the middle of their foreheads. When you walk to the market, you find someone is making fun of this. Talk to the person and explain the dot's significance. *R–cu*

4. You are concerned about your safety in the US because you have heard that many Americans do not like foreigners. You've heard that several tourists have been killed for their money and cars. Talk to an American friend and find out if your fears are founded. *R–cu*

5. You are at a birthday party and you notice that everyone else has brought a gift. You did not know this was the custom. Talk to the person whose birthday it is. *R–cu*

6. You were invited to a "pot luck" and you thought "pot luck" was just another name for a party. Unfortunately, you didn't know that everyone brings a different dish to this kind of party. Apologize to your host for not bringing anything and explain your misunderstanding. *R–cu*

7. An American friend is getting married next weekend and you are invited to the wedding. You are planning to bring all your relatives (your mother, father, three brothers, two sisters, your grandmother and your aunt) because you know your relatives would like to meet your friend. Discuss your plans with someone else who is invited to the wedding to see if what you are planning to do is appropriate. *R–cu*

8. You have just met someone and this person is asking you a lot of personal questions. In your country, this would be rude. You are very uncomfortable. Talk to this person about how you are feeling. *R–cu*

9. You are going dancing with several of your friends. You arrive at the club in very formal wear, while your friends (and everyone else at the club) are dressed in jeans and T-shirts. You feel embarrassed and want to go home. Talk to your friend about what to do. *R–cu*

10. You were taught that it is impolite to look directly at someone when you do not know that person well. A friend of yours thinks you don't like him because you don't look at him when he speaks to you. Talk to your friend and explain your custom. *R–cu*

11. You are at a party where everyone brought something to eat. Your friend brought a typical dish from her country. It looks and smells rather odd, and no one at the party wants to try it. People are laughing and talking about how bad the dish smells and your friend looks upset. Talk to her. *R–cu*

12. You were invited to a "costume" party, but you thought it was a "customs party". When you arrive, everyone except you is dressed up in costume. Tell your host that you would like to go home. *R–cu*

13. As you are walking to your neighborhood drug store, you see a circle of people holding signs and shouting for you not to go into the store. Ask someone what is going on and what you should do. *R–cu*

14. An American friend asks you why people in your country are not very clean. At first you are insulted, but you would like to explain that the custom in your country is to take long hot baths once or twice a week, rather than taking short showers daily. Talk to your friend about the different bathing customs. *R–cu*

15. You notice your friend does not lock her door when she leaves her room. When you ask why she explains that this is the custom in her country. Tell her that she must learn to lock her door now because it is unsafe to do otherwise. *R–cu*

16. Your new American friends come to visit you and bring a bottle of alcohol. They want to toast your new home, but you have never tasted alcohol because it is against your religion. Explain why you have refused the glass offered to you. *R–cu*

17. Some of your classmates laugh when you speak English. You know you have an accent and you make mistakes, but you want to keep trying. Talk to one of your classmates and explain how you are feeling. *R–cu*

18. In your country, people never talk about sex in public. In this country you find that all people talk about is sex, sex, sex. Discuss this with someone else from your country. *R–cu*

19. A friend of yours tells you your clothing is not fashionable and you need to "Americanize" your wardrobe. Tell your friend that you do not want to be "Americanized" and that you are comfortable with yourself the way you are. *R–cu*

20. You want very much to fit in with the American lifestyle. Your best friend wants you to get a tattoo. You are afraid to do this, but you don't want your friend to know that. What do you say to your friend? *R–cu*

21. You and your friends are always teasing each other. However, today you made a sarcastic comment about someone from another country because you thought it was funny. Now this person is very upset. Talk to this person about it.   *R–cu*

22. You were invited to a formal party, and you asked a friend to come with you. Unfortunately, you said, "Let's have an affair together" instead of "Let's go to an affair together." Now you are embarrassed to talk to your friend. Be brave and explain the misunderstanding.   *R–cu*

23. In your native country students are very quiet and do not ask any questions. Now you are studying in the US, and a friend asks why you never participate. What do you say?   *R–cu*

24. You went to the Employment Development office to find out if they could help you find a job. You wanted to dress for an interview, so you are wearing an outfit that you usually wear to church. Your friends are laughing at you and telling you you are overdressed. Talk to your friend about what outfit would be more appropriate.   *R–cu*

Dating

1. Your boyfriend from your hometown is visiting you. Explain to him that you have been dating someone else.   *R-da*

2. A woman is continually inviting you to go out with her, but you don't like her at all. Ask her to leave you alone.   *R-da*

3. Tell your boyfriend that you are pregnant and discuss your options.   *R-da*

4. Your girlfriend wants to elope but you don't. Explain your reasons. Try to dissuade her.   *R-da*

5. Tell your fiancé that you want to call off your engagement.   *R-da*

6. Try to get your friend to propose to you.   *R-da*

7. Your lover wants to marry you, but you aren't sure. Talk to your best friend about it.   *R-da*

8. You are in love. Ask your friend to marry you.   *R-da*

9. Ask your friend about married life. Explain to your friend that you are interested in getting married, but you aren't sure if you are ready for a commitment.*R-da*

10. You have made a first date with a person whom you really would like to impress. You promised to take your date to a concert, but you are unable to find the concert tickets. Explain this problem to your date.   *R-da*

11. You want to go out with a friend of yours but want to be sure that your friend understands that you are each going to pay for your own dinners. Talk about it.   *R-da*

12. Talk to the father of the woman whom you would like to marry. Ask for his blessings.   *R-da*

13. You meet your blind date at a coffee shop. You are shocked because he looks nothing like the way he was described to you. Talk to your date. *R-da*

14. Your date believes in sex on the first date and you don't. Discuss your different opinions on this subject. *R-da*

15. Your friend has invited you out and takes you to a very expensive restaurant. When the bill comes, she tells you that your half comes to $55. Tell her that you thought she was going to pay, and that you didn't bring enough cash. *R-da*

16. Your best friend is dating someone you really like. Talk to your friend. *R-da*

17. You saw your boyfriend with another woman and you are feeling very jealous. Talk to him about this. *R-da*

18. Your fiancé wants to have a big wedding, but you want to have a small, intimate one. Discuss it. Compromise. Work it out. *R-da*

19. You have discovered that your girlfriend has lied to you about where she was last night. Confront her with this. *R-da*

20. Whenever you and your friend are on a date, your friend talks about past loves. Talk to your friend about this. *R-da*

21. You want to have a child but you don't want to get married. Ask a friend to be the father of a child for you. *R-da*

22. Your friend wants you to help her get a date. You don't want to get involved. Tell her this. *R-da*

23. Your friend wants to know why he doesn't have many dates. Explain gently that he should do something about his appearance. *R-da*

24. You and your date run into a friend of yours. Not only does your friend invite himself to join you, but you think he is flirting with your date. When your date goes to the restroom, confront your friend with your suspicions. *R-da*

25. You and your friend usually stay home on weekends and watch TV together. You would like to go out more often. Talk to your friend about this. *R-da*

26. Your friend is from another country and is uncomfortable about dating. Talk to your friend about dating customs. *R-da*

27. You want to advertise for a date in the personal column of the newspaper, but you don't know what to say. Ask a friend to help you with wording your ad. *R-da*

28. You find that you are always paying for the dates you and your friend have. Talk to your friend about this. *R-da*

29. You want to have a lot of children but your lover doesn't want to have any. Tell your lover that you think this difference may put an end to your relationship. *R-da*

30. You are on your first date with a friend whom you really like. All of a sudden, you feel ill. When you tell her this she thinks you are making it up because you don't like her. Convince her that you're telling the truth. *R-da*

31. Try to get a person whom you hardly know to ask you out on a date.   *R-da*

32. You want to go home but your date wants to stay out all night and dance with you.   *R-da*

33. Try to convince your date to go to a party. He does not want to go because he feels he will not know anyone there.   *R-da*

34. Your parent does not like the friend you are going out with. Tell your parent what a good person your friend is.   *R-da*

35. You are coming to pick up your date. Your date's mother answers the door, and it is obvious that she doesn't like you. Try to be friendly.   *R-da*

36. You are on a date and you think your date is flirting with someone else. Tell your date to stop doing this.   *R-da*

37. Try to get a friend of yours to go out with another friend of yours on a blind date.   *R-da*

38. Your friend is very possessive of you. Explain to your friend that you are the type of person who doesn't like to be tied down. *R-da*

39. When you introduce your date to your best friend, you have the distinct impression that they knew each other. Find out from your friend if this is true.   *R-da*

40. Tell your friend that you don't like his girlfriend.   *R-da*

41. Explain to your best friend that the new person she is dating is someone you used to date. *R-da*

42. Tell your friend that you are in love with his girlfriend.   *R-da*

43. Tell your platonic friend that you are becoming sexually attracted to him.   *R-da*

44. You think your date is chauvinistic. Talk to him about his attitude.   *R-da*

45. Your date tells you that she thinks money is not important for happiness. You think it is very necessary. Discuss the relationship between money and happiness.   *R-da*

46. Your friends are always talking about sex. You feel uncomfortable and left out because you know you want to be a virgin when you marry, and you don't understand why everyone has to brag about who did what to whom. Talk to a friend about how you feel.   *R-da*

47. You and your friend have been dating for some time. Tell your friend that you do not want to have sex with him.   *R-da*

48. You are on a date and having a terrible time. Ask your date to take you home.   *R-da*

49. You are on your first date and have parked to watch the moon and the stars. You begin kissing, and after a while you ask your date to stop. Instead, your date laughs at you and says you are a tease. Convince your date that you mean what you say.   *R-da*

50. You are on a date with a woman who can't seem to take her hands off you. You are finding this embarrassing. Talk to her and explain how you feel.   *R-da*

51. Ask a man you really like to go out on a date with you.   *R-da*

52. You are on a date with a person who seems to only want to talk about himself. Talk to him about this. *R-da*

53. You are living with your girlfriend and decide that the arrangement is just not working. Talk to her. *R-da*

54. At a restaurant, your date has ordered the most expensive items on the menu. You think she is only interested in you for your money. Talk it out. *R-da*

55. Your date asks you if she could borrow $200 from you. What do you say? *R-da*

56. Your date seems to only be interested in impressing you. Talk to your date about this. *R-da*

57. Tell your friend that either you both make a commitment and start living together or your relationship is over. *R-da*

58. Tell your lover that your past partner has tested positive for HIV, the AIDS virus. Ask your lover to go to the clinic with you so you can both be tested. *R-da*

59. Talk to your date about having safe sex. *R-da*

60. Tell your lover that you have been unfaithful. *R-da*

Descriptions

1. Although you promised to meet your friend at the airport at 8 o'clock, there was so much traffic that you didn't arrive until 9:30. You and your friend were supposed to meet at the baggage claim area, but only an attendant is there now. Ask the attendant what happened to your friend. *R-de*

2. Someone just stole your wallet. Go to the police station and describe the person that you think stole it. *R-de*

3. When you were looking out your window, you saw someone leaning against your car. When you went to your car half an hour later, the automobile had vanished. Describe the person whom you saw near your car to the police. *R-de*

4. Ask your friend if she has seen your sister. She was supposed to meet you in front of your house at 3:00. It is now 5:00. *R-de*

5. Your friend wants to know all about the people in your class. Describe them. *R-de*

6. You meet a tourist on the bus. Describe the nicest part of this city to him. *R-de*

7. Describe some of the teachers at this school to a student who used to go here. This student is very bad with names and can't remember his former teachers. Find out if this person had any of the teachers that you have now. *R-de*

8. You have just seen a person set fire to a building. The police come. Describe the person you saw to the police. *R-de*

9. Your friend is blind. The two of you go to the beach at sunset. Describe for your friend what you see. *R-de*

10. Someone on the bus dropped her wallet as she left the bus. Tell the bus driver and describe the person to the driver. *R-de*

11. Someone was following you home last night. Tell the police and describe the person. *R-de*

12. Describe your sister to someone who wants to meet her. *R-de*

13. You just met the most attractive person you have ever seen. Tell your friend what this person looked like. *R-de*

14. Your lover is in your native country, and you are homesick. Tell your friend about the person you miss. *R-de*

15. Your friend wants you to double date with another person. Ask your friend to describe your date and then you will make your decision. *R-de*

16. Describe your apartment to your friend. *R-de*

17. You are crazy about someone but you don't want anyone to know who this person is. Tell your friend about your secret love without using any names. *R-de*

18. Someone came up to you, bumped you and took your wallet. Although it happened very quickly, you must describe this person to a police officer. *R-de*

19. Your friend has not been at home or at work for two days. You are concerned. Go to the police and find out what to do to file a missing person's report. *R-de*

20. You saw a small child wandering alone in the park. Tell a police officer. *R-de*

21. You saw your friend walking arm in arm with somebody you have never seen before. When you ask your friend to tell you about this, your friend doesn't know who you are talking about. Describe the person you saw your friend walking with so that your friend will remember the incident. *R-de*

22. Tell your friend about someone you met at a bar last night. *R-de*

23. Tell your friend about a very quiet place where you go to feel at peace with nature. *R-de*

24. Describe the people in your family to your friend, and find out who in your friend's family your friend looks like. *R-de*

25. You met someone who is moving and leaving an apartment in the city. Since you are looking for a place to live, ask this person to describe the apartment to you. *R-de*

26. Your cat is missing. Ask your neighbor if he has seen it. *R-de*

27. Your friend tells you that she is going to get married. Ask her to tell you about her fiancé. *R-de*

28. Describe the nicest place in your native country. *R-de*

29. You went to a bar with a friend. The two of you got separated. Ask someone if they have seen your friend anywhere. *R-de*

30. You call up a blind date. Ask her what she looks like and describe yourself. *R-de*

31. Your friend just bought a new house. Find out about the house and how your friend found it. *R-de*

32. You met a very nice person at a café last night. You have gone to the café again hoping to see that person again. Ask a waiter if the person you met yesterday has been there today. *R-de*

33. You are in a shopping mall and you can't find your friend. Describe your friend and ask people if they've seen anyone matching that description. *R-de*

34. A child in your neighborhood is missing. You have volunteered to ask people in your community if they've seen the child. Talk to a neighbor. *R-de*

Directions (Getting)

1. You need to meet someone at a shop and you are lost and it is late. Ask someone on the street to help you. *R-dgt*

2. Ask someone to explain how to get to the nearest bank. *R-dgt*

3. Ask your friend to explain to you how to get to the library. *R-dgt*

4. Ask for directions to the nearest supermarket. *R-dgt*

5. You have been driving for nearly an hour when your car breaks down. Stop someone on the highway and ask where you can find a mechanic. *R-dgt*

6. You are on the wrong bus. Ask the driver how you can get back to where you need to go. *R-dgt*

7. You need to pay a traffic ticket. You are at the courthouse and do not know where to go. Ask someone for help. *R-dgt*

8. Find out the directions to a thrift shop in your neighborhood. *R-dgt*

9. You have to get your gas and electricity started. Ask your friend where you need to go. *R-dgt*

10. When you find out your family is coming to visit you, you need to make hotel reservations quickly. Find out where the best hotels are in this city. *R-dgt*

11. You were supposed to meet your friend at a specific street corner. After waiting half an hour, you ask someone on the street if you are at the right corner. This person tells you that there is another corner that meets your description and that perhaps you should go there. Ask the person to direct you. *R-dgt*

12. You have never been to your date's house before. Find out how to get there. *R-dgt*

13. You are looking to buy a used car. Call up a person whose name you found in the paper. Ask for directions to so that you can go over and see the car. *R-dgt*

14. Ask a waiter at a restaurant where the bathroom is. You looked but you couldn't find it. Look and then ask again. *R-dgt*

15. Find out where you can go to look for inexpensive housing. *R-dgt*

16. Your friend has had too much to drink. You have taken the car keys from him and would like to drive him home. Find out where the car is parked.   *R-dgt*

17. A friend is going to take a cruise. You have come to see your friend off, but can't find the right pier. Ask someone to help you. *R-dgt*

18. You are hungry, lost, and have little money. Find out where you can go to get a free hot meal and ask how to get there.   *R-dgt*

19. A child comes up to you and tells you she is lost. See if you can help her find her house.   *R-dgt*

20. A new club opened in your neighborhood. Ask a friend where it is.   *R-dgt*

21. You were supposed to meet your friend at church. You thought you knew where the church was, but when you arrived you realized you were not at the right one. Stop someone and get directions to the correct church.   *R-dgt*

Directions (Giving)

1. You are driving and you suddenly get a flat tire. You do not have a spare. Call a garage and explain where you are.   *R-dgv*

2. Your friend is coming to visit you from another country. You will be in school when your friend arrives. Explain how to get to the school.   *R-dgv*

3. Your friend wants to meet you at a movie theater but does not know where it is. Explain how to get there.   *R-dgv*

4. Your friend has just bought a car but is very nervous about driving it. He wants to make sure he knows how to get to your house. Go over the directions with him.   *R-dgv*

5. You are out on a date. You and your friend need to pick up another couple. Direct your date to their house from yours.   *R-dgv*

6. Your friend wants to meet you at a restaurant. Explain where it is.   *R-dgv*

7. You meet an old friend of yours on the street. Tell her about your new apartment and explain where it is.   *R-dgv*

8. You have rearranged all the furniture in your house. You meet your friend at a coffee shop. Explain to your friend how you arranged the furniture.   *R-dgv*

9. You have an ad in the paper for a babysitter. Explain to a prospective sitter where you live and how to get there.   *R-dgv*

10. You are at the information desk of a hospital working as a volunteer. An old woman who has trouble hearing asks you where the Family Gift Shop is.   *R-dgv*

11. A tourist is on a bus with you. He is looking at a map of the city. Ask if you can help him.   *R-dgv*

12. Your friend would like to take a bus to see you over the holidays. Explain to your friend how to get to your house from the bus station.   *R-dgv*

13. Someone you met needs a place to stay for the night. Explain how to get to your place. *R-dgv*

14. Help a friend plan a vacation to your city. Tell your friend where to go and what to see. *R-dgv*

15. You are planning a surprise anniversary party for your parents. Explain to a relative how to get to the party. *R-dgv*

16. You are working in a department store and a customer asks you where to go for some good music. *R-dgv*

17. Your friend wants to work out at the gym you frequent. You have a guest pass. Tell your friend how to get there and where to meet you. *R-dgv*

18. You are ordering some flowers. Explain to the florist where to deliver them. *R-dgv*

19. Order a pizza and ask for it to be delivered to your house. Explain how to get there. *R-dgv*

20. You are having a garage sale at a friend's house. Explain to someone how to get there. *R-dgv*

Emotions/Feelings

1. Your friend is very impatient. Tell him that you think this is a very bad characteristic. Talk about different ways of passing the time while waiting. *R-ef*

2. You have a very bad temper. Ask your friend what she does when angry. *R-ef*

3. Find out why your partner gets so moody. *R-ef*

4. Your friend is very upset about something but won't tell you what the matter is. Try to comfort her. *R-ef*

5. Your friend is in a really bad mood. Try to cheer your friend up. *R-ef*

6. Talk to your partner about the things which irritate you and how to avoid these things. *R-ef*

7. Find out what kinds of things make your partner nervous. Discuss various ways to calm down. *R-ef*

8. Ask a friend why he is always alone. *R-ef*

9. Ask your partner what things frighten him. Find out what he does when he is afraid. *R-ef*

10. Ask your partner if he thinks it's better to hold in anger or to release it. Share a couple of your experiences to explain your opinion on this. *R-ef*

11. Tell your partner you feel lonely and homesick. *R-ef*

12. You feel very bad about an argument you had with an old friend. Now your friend refuses to talk to you. Try to apologize for what you said in anger. *R-ef*

13. Your friend is very shy and nervous when there are new people around. Talk to him about ways to conquer his fears. *R-ef*

14. Your friend seems very nervous about something. Find out what the problem is. *R-ef*

15. Your friend becomes violent when she is angry, and you are worried that she might strike her children. Find out if she might consider attending an anger-management program. *R-ef*

16. Your friend is about to get married. He is very nervous. Calm him down. *R-ef*

17. Your friend has very little self-confidence. You would like to help her gain confidence. What can you say? *R-ef*

18. Ask your friend to forgive you for saying something nasty to him in anger. *R-ef*

19. Apologize for throwing something at your friend. Explain that you have a bad temper and must learn how to control it. *R-ef*

20. Your friend never shows any emotion. Tell her that you think this is unhealthy. *R-ef*

21. You are worried about your friend because he seems very depressed. Talk to him about seeing a counselor. *R-ef*

22. You have begun to notice that a good friend has very abrupt mood swings. Try to convince your friend to get some help. *R-ef*

23. A parent of one of your friends has just died. Try to console your friend. *R-ef*

24. Your friend was in a terrible motorcycle accident. Talk to your friend's mother. *R-ef*

25. Your dog has just been hit by a car and is at the veterinary hospital. Talk to your friend about whether you should have the dog put to sleep. *R-ef*

26. Your partner seems to take everything very seriously and has become very emotional lately. Find out what the matter is. *R-ef*

27. A good friend of yours has been talking a lot about death. You are worried that your friend may do something terrible. Talk to your friend. *R-ef*

28. Someone you know has had an abortion. She has not told any of her friends. Try to talk to her about what she has been going through. *R-ef*

29. A neighbor of yours has just given birth to a baby with Down's Syndrome. You would like to help her with the baby, but you feel awkward because you don't know whether to congratulate the mother or not. Talk to her. *R-ef*

30. Your sister was pregnant and has just miscarried. She is acting as if nothing happened. Talk to her and try to get her to open up about her feelings. *R-ef*

31. A friend of yours adopted a child not too long ago. He has found out that the birth parents are going to contest the adoption. Try to comfort him and cheer him up. *R-ef*

32. You have a friend who always seems to be happy. Find out how he does it. *R-ef*

33. Your sister asks for a lot from your parents, and she seems to get everything she wants. You resent this and want to bring your feelings out in the open. Tell her how you feel. *R-ef*

34. You are attending the funeral of your uncle. Go over and comfort your aunt. *R-ef*

35. You have seen the way your friend neglects his aging parents. You find his behavior appalling. Tell him so.   *R-ef*

36. You have waited a long time to tell your best friend that you are gay. You are worried about how your friend will react. Explain to your friend how you feel and why it took you so long to talk about it.   *R-ef*

37. Your father's friend has just told you that he is in love with you and has been for years. What do you say to him?   *R-ef*

38. All your life you have been teased because you could not learn as quickly as other people. You get frustrated easily and have trouble dealing with your emotions. Visit a counselor and ask for advice.   *R-ef*

39. You are very sensitive to other people but find that others are continually hurting your feelings. Talk to a counselor about how to protect yourself from feeling so bad.   *R-ef*

40. A friend of yours has told you that you are whiny and obnoxious. Tell your friend that you are just being who you are, and tell your friend that you can't do anything about it.   *R-ef*

41. You just witnessed several teenagers making fun of a very fat person who has fallen in the street. Talk to the person and ask if you can help.   *R-ef*

42. Your friend is very sensitive about losing his hair. He wears a hat all the time and refuses to take it off. Talk to him.   *R-ef*

43. You have a friend who has been on every known diet but is unable to lose weight. Your friend is very unhappy and frustrated. Try to comfort your friend and sympathize.   *R-ef*

44. You have a friend who is in a wheelchair. Your friend feels that everyone stares, but no one talks to him. Try to make him feel better about his situation.   *R-ef*

45. Many of your friends were invited to a party, but you were not. You are feeling left out. Ask one of your friends who was invited why you were not.   *R-ef*

46. Your friend has just been in an automobile accident and is upset. Practice good listening. Don't try to fix the situation, just be empathetic.   *R-ef*

47. Your grandmother asked you to come over because she says you never come by and she is lonely. Talk to her.   *R-ef*

Explanations

1. Your friend is having a party. Suggest a game to play and explain how to play it.   *R-ex*

2. Explain to your friend how to meet a member of the opposite sex.   *R-ex*

3. Your friend is having trouble with someone who likes him. This person has been following him around wherever he goes. Explain to your friend what he ought to do.   *R-ex*

4. Explain how to do something that you do well.   *R-ex*

5. Your friend needs to borrow some money. Explain how she can get get a loan.   *R-ex*

6. Your friend has a garden which is not doing well. Explain how to care for plants.   *R-ex*

7. Your friend usually drinks too much at parties, all kinds of parties. Explain how to drink without getting drunk.   *R-ex*

8. Your friend is in love with someone who does not reciprocate. Explain how to get someone to love you.   *R-ex*

9. Explain how your friend needs to act in order to be more friendly.   *R-ex*

10. Your friend has been rejected by a member of the opposite sex. Explain how to get over a broken heart.   *R-ex*

11. Your friend always gets a bad sunburn when he goes out to the beach. Explain how to get a good tan without getting burnt.   *R-ex*

12. You and your friend are going skiing this weekend. Your friend has never skied before. Explain to your friend how to pack for the trip and what equipment you will be needing.   *R-ex*

13. Explain to your parents why you are joining the Peace Corps. *R-ex*

14. Explain to your friend why you need to copy his homework. *R-ex*

15. A friend of yours is having trouble disciplining her two-year-old twins. Explain what to do.   *R-ex*

16. Explain to your parents why you want to move out.   *R-ex*

17. Explain to your partner why you need more space in your relationship.   *R-ex*

18. Explain how to cook something easy but impressive.   *R-ex*

19. Explain how to drive a car with a stick shift to someone who has only driven an automatic.   *R-ex*

20. Explain how to study for a test.   *R-ex*

21. Your friend has trouble saving money. Explain how to budget money so that your friend can save.   *R-ex*

22. It takes you forever to clean your house. Your friend cleans house very quickly. Ask if there are some tricks you can learn. *R-ex*

23. Ask a friend how to buy a good used car.   *R-ex*

24. Explain to your friend how to find an apartment.   *R-ex*

25. Explain to your friend how to make new friends in a foreign country.   *R-ex*

26. Ask your friend to explain to you the process involved in learning English.   *R-ex*

27. Explain to your friend the things you must do if you want to get along with a roommate.   *R-ex*

28. Your friend hasn't been feeling very well. Explain how to stay fit and healthy.   *R-ex*

29. You and your friend are at a swap meet. Explain how to look for antiques and how to bargain with the seller to lower the price.   *R-ex*

30. Explain how to furnish an new apartment inexpensively.   *R-ex*

31. Ask your friend how to make your wardrobe seem larger without spending a lot of money.   *R-ex*

32. Explain to your friend how to take better care of her car.   *R-ex*

33. Explain the steps involved in getting married in your home country.   *R-ex*

34. Explain to your friend how to marry someone with a lot of money.   *R-ex*

35. Your friend wants to lose weight. Explain how to do this safely.   *R-ex*

36. Your friend wants to stop smoking. Explain what must be done to accomplish this.   *R-ex*

37. Explain to a friend who is on a tourist visa how to become a US citizen.   *R-ex*

38. Explain to a new friend how to register for a Social Security card.   *R-ex*

39. A friend has just lost his job. Explain how your friend can get unemployment benefits.   *R-ex*

40. Your friend is out of work and is struggling to make ends meet. Explain to your friend how to get public assistance.   *R-ex*

41. You are on a committee to help keep our streets clean. Explain how to accomplish this.   *R-ex*

42. You were just in an automobile accident. Go to your insurance company, explain what happened and find out what to do.   *R-ex*

43. Ask a divorced friend what you must do to get a divorce.   *R-ex*

44. Explain to someone who just arrived in this country how to act friendly but not too friendly to strangers.   *R-ex*

Famous People

1. Talk to the President of the United States. Tell him that you disagree with the way he is handling the economy.   *R-fp*

2. Talk to Princess Diana. Ask her what it's like to be constantly in the tabloid newspapers.   *R-fp*

3. Talk to Mother Teresa about her visions of world peace.   *R-fp*

4. Ask Arnold Schwartzenegger how he learned English so well.   *R-fp*

5. Thank Alexander Graham Bell for the telephone. Tell him how useful it has become.   *R-fp*

6. Ask Martha Washington how she feels about the changes in American women.   *R-fp*

7. Talk to John F. Kennedy. Ask him who he thinks assassinated him.   *R-fp*

8. Talk to Martin Luther King, Jr. Ask him why he was killed.   *R-fp*

9. Ask Rock Hudson why he didn't disclose that he had AIDS.   *R-fp*

10. Introduce yourself to Oprah Winfrey. Ask her about her ideas on the equality of the sexes.   *R-fp*

11. Find out from Mickey Mouse how he has stayed so young looking. *R-fp*

12. Tell Rush Limbaugh that he has a big mouth. *R-fp.*

13. Talk to Elvis Presley. Ask him what he thinks of Michael Jackson. *R-fp*

14. Ask Albert Einstein why he had so much trouble in school. *R-fp*

15. Ask Dr.Spock how he thinks people should raise their children. *R-fp*

16. Ask Madonna what she believes in. Ask her if she takes herself seriously. *R-fp*

17. Tell Dr. Sigmund Freud that you've been having some problems recently. *R-fp*

18. Ask Santa Claus why it is important for children to know about him. *R-fp*

19. Ask Captain Kirk what it's like to travel to different planets. *R-fp*

20. Convince Mozart to give you music lessons. *R-fp*

21. Ask Picasso his views on the purpose of art. *R-fp*

22. Find out why Superman feels that he must continually fight crime. *R-fp*

23. Ask Don Juan why he needs so many girlfriends. *R-fp*

24. Tell Alfred Hitchcock that you don't like his films. *R-fp*

25. Talk to Abraham Lincoln. Ask him if he thinks he should be a hero. *R-fp*

26. Ask The Beauty what she sees in The Beast. *R-fp*

27. Ask the founder of Kentucky Fried Chicken, Colonel Sanders, how he got started in the chicken business. *R-fp*

28. Ask Mick Jagger what his plans for the future are. *R-fp*

29. Find out from Elizabeth Taylor how to interest a man. *R-fp*

30. Ask the Devil if she exists within all people. *R-fp*

31. Ask John Lennon why the Beatles really broke up. *R-fp*

32. Ask Sting if that's his real name and what it means. *R-fp*

33. Ask Cinderella if people can really live happily ever after. *R-fp*

34. Find out if Dorothy is still in Kansas, and what she has been doing since the movie "The Wizard of Oz". *R-fp*

35. Ask Big Bird if he feels threatened by Barney. *R-fp*

36. Ask Caesar if Cleopatra's beauty was worth dying for. *R-fp*

37. Ask Adonis how he stays so physically fit. *R-fp*

38. Ask Joan of Arc why she was willing to sacrifice herself. *R-fp*

39. Ask Josephine why she married Napoleon. *R-fp*

40. Find out why Peter Pan never wanted to grow up. *R-fp*

41. Ask Cinderella how she and Prince Charming are doing after all these years. *R-fp*

42. Talk to John Wayne about his relationship with his horse. *R-fp*

43. Find out if Christopher Columbus has any doubts today about what he did. *R-fp*

44. Ask Jesus Christ how he would reach people today. *R-fp*

45. Ask the Three Bears how they feel about Goldilocks. *R-fp*

46. Ask Confucius what he thinks of fortune cookies. *R-fp*

47. Ask James Bond if you can help him on his next mission. *R-fp*

Health

1. You are visiting a friend in the hospital who is gravely ill. He does not realize how sick he is. Talk to him. *R-he*

2. You have come to see your friend who is in the hospital. Ask the nurse how your friend is doing. *R-he*

3. You feel sick. Ask your friend to help you get to the doctor. *R-he*

4. You are in the hospital. You are worried because you are going to have surgery. Talk to the nurse about it. *R-he*

5. You go to the emergency room because you are not feeling very well. You have been waiting a long time. Ask the receptionist how much longer it will be. *R-he*

6. You have just been wheeled into a hospital room. Talk to the person in the next bed. *R-he*

7. You have been very nervous and depressed lately. Ask your doctor if something can be prescribed for you. *R-he*

8. The dentist tells you that the work you need is going to be very expensive. Find out if you can pay in installments. *R-he*

9. Your friend is very sick but refuses to go to the doctor. Try to convince your friend to make an appointment. *R-he*

10. One of your children is sexually active and you are concerned about the risk of AIDS. Ask your doctor for advice on how to discuss this with your child. *R-he*

11. You have had a runny nose, sore throat and muscle aches for several weeks. The doctor told you it was nothing. Talk to the doctor again and explain that you think it is more serious. *R-he*

12. You go to the dentist because you have a bad toothache. The dentist tells you your tooth must be pulled out immediately. Explain to your dentist that you would like to get a second opinion. *R-he*

13. You are scheduled to have an operation shortly. You are in a hospital room and the patient next to you tells you that the hospital has been on the news because of several law suits involving negligence. Find out more about this. *R-he*

14. Your doctor tells you that you need to have surgery. You don't want to have it. Talk about the options. *R-he*

15. Your best friend needs to have an operation, but your friend's religion won't permit it. Talk to your friend about the consequences. *R-he*

16. You've just hurt yourself playing soccer, but you feel your team needs you. The coach tells you to get off the field, but you still want to be in the game. Talk to your coach.   *R-he*

17. While your friend is recuperating in the hospital, his house is robbed. No one has said anything to your friend yet, but you feel he needs to know. Tell him.   *R-he*

18. You are losing your hair and are afraid of going totally bald. Ask your doctor to prescribe something to restore your lost hair.   *R-he*

19. Last night you had unprotected sex and you are afraid that you might be pregnant or have gotten AIDS. Ask your doctor what you can do.   *R-he*

20. Tell your doctor that you would like to have some type of birth control. Find out what is available.   *R-he*

21. Your friend tested HIV positive and asked you not to tell anyone. There is a new man in your friend's life, and you are worried that your friend may not have told him that she is positive. Talk to her about telling her new beau about her illness.   *R-he*

22. You are worried because you have not been feeling well for some time. You are afraid to go to the doctor but you are thinking you might be HIV positive. Talk to a friend.   *R-he*

23. You have discovered that you have a sexually transmitted disease. Talk to your lover and convince that person to see a doctor.   *R-he*

24. Your sister has been losing more and more weight. She is now extremely thin but says she is still fat. Talk to her about seeing a doctor.   *R-he*

25. Your friend is concerned he might be impotent, but he is embarrassed to talk to his doctor. Convince your friend to get a check-up.   *R-he*

26. You suspect that a patient of yours has been beaten by her lover. She is in the hospital and is refusing to talk about what happened. You know she is very afraid. Talk to her.   *R-he*

27. A good friend of yours is very depressed after an ugly divorce. Your friend does not believe in psychologists or psychiatrists. Try to talk to your friend about seeing someone who can help.   *R-he*

28. Your friend has been seeing a homeopathic doctor for several months, but does not appear to be getting any healthier. Talk to your friend.   *R-he*

29. Your friend has always had many physical problems. Recently your friend has become involved with yoga and meditation and believes that physical health is completely controlled by the mind. Find out if these activities have improved your friend's health.   *R-he*

30. You are having back pain. Talk to a friend about seeing an acupuncturist.   *R-he*

31. Your friend believes in taking megadoses of vitamins to prevent illness. Talk to your friend about this.   *R-he*

32. The mother of a friend of yours has cancer but refuses to do chemotherapy. Talk to her. *R-he*

33. Your friend is overweight, does not exercise and smokes cigarettes. Tell him you are concerned for his health. *R-he*

34. Talk to your doctor about alternative medicine. *R-he*

35. Your friend has a heart condition but wants to live life to its fullest. Talk to your friend about moderation. *R-he*

36. You are pregnant with triplets. Your doctor informs you that having triplets could be dangerous to your health as well as the babies. Talk to your doctor about what you can do. *R-he*

37. You have had a very premature baby who weighs only a pound and a half. Talk to a nurse in the neonatal intensive care unit about the progress of your newborn. *R-he*

38. An elderly relative of yours is in great pain and doesn't want to live anymore. Talk to your relative. *R-he*

39. Your friend is ill but has no money for health insurance and is afraid to go to the doctor. Talk to your friend. *R-he*

40. Your parent is on life support. The doctors tell you there is no hope and want to know if they should stop life support. Talk to a doctor about this. *R-he*

41. You cannot decide whether to bottlefeed or breastfeed your baby. Talk to a lactation nurse about the pros and cons. *R-he*

42. You think one of your parents may be seriously ill but is avoiding going to the doctor. Ask the doctor what you can do. *R-he*

43. Your parents are concerned that if one of them gets sick and needs to be in a nursing home, it will be so expensive that it will wipe out their entire life savings. Talk about these concerns to one of your parents. *R-he*

44. You need to find a nursing home for an elderly relative. Talk to the head of a local home and find out about the care there. *R-he*

45. Your friend is a vegetarian and feels that people should eat only organic vegetables. You eat everything and don't worry about your health. Talk to your friend about nutrition. *R-he*

46. You are concerned because your partner spends quite a lot of time working out at the gym. You feel that your partner is overdoing it and that this is unwise. Discuss it. *R-he*

47. You are looking for a good doctor for your child, but you don't know the difference between a general practitioner or a pediatrician, or a nurse practitioner and a physician's assistant. Ask your friend to help you decide. *R-he*

48. Talk to a doctor at your local clinic. Find out if this doctor would be appropriate for your family. *R-he*

49. Talk to your friend about getting life insurance so that your friend's family is protected. *R-he*

50. Discuss with your friend what to do in the event of an earthquake. *R-he*

51. Your friend is critically ill but would like to die at home rather than in a hospital bed. Talk to the hospital counselor about hospice care.   *R-he*

52. You are nervous. Ask a friend to go with you when you have your first mammogram.   *R-he*

53. Tell your doctor about your family history and ask her to give you a blood test to screen for prostate cancer.   *R-he*

54. You are having trouble sleeping. Ask your doctor to suggest something that can help you sleep at night.   *R-he*

55. Your friend is constantly complaining of various medical problems. Tell your friend to stop spending so much time focusing on these ailments.   *R-he*

56. Your friend seems to always have an ailment and needs to see a doctor. You believe your friend is a hypochondriac. Talk to your friend about seeing a psychologist rather than a physician.   *R-he*

57. A good friend has just died, and you would like to attend the funeral. Find out from another friend what you should wear and what would be appropriate to bring for the family.   *R-he*

58. You are seventeen years old and considering having sex for the first time. Talk to your family doctor about birth control.   *R-he*

59. Your teenage child has always confided in you. Suddenly last week, your child seemed to be sick and wouldn't talk to you. Try to find out what's wrong.   *R-he*

60. You are fifteen years old and pregnant. Your boyfriend and you have not decided what to do, whether to have the baby and keep it, put it up for adoption, or abort the fetus. Talk to someone at Planned Parenthood about your options.   *R-he*

61. You would like to adopt a child who suffers from Fetal Alcohol Syndrome. Talk to a counselor and find out what you can expect from this child and what problems you must be prepared to deal with.   *R-he*

62. For several years you have known your child not only had many difficulties learning, but also expressed a violent temper. The doctor has finally diagnosed your child with Attention Deficit Disorder. Find out from your doctor what can be done to help your child.   *R-he*

63. Even though you knew you were pregnant, you took some illegal drugs and drank alcohol. Now that your baby is born, you are worried about the effects of your behavior on the baby's development. You are afraid to tell the doctor because you don't want to get into trouble. Talk to a friend about what to do.   *R-he*

64. Your parent is elderly and starting to forget things. Ask the doctor what you can do about it, and whether your parent could have Alzheimer's.   *R-he*

65. You were told by your lover that you sleepwalk at night. Ask your doctor what you can do.   *R-he*

66. Your father seems old and tired today. Ask what's wrong.   *R-he*

67. Talk to a mortician about funeral arrangements for a friend.   *R-he*

68. A loved one told you that you have a drinking problem and made you promise to see a doctor. You feel you can stop drinking at any time, and you do not have a problem. Talk to the doctor.   *R-he*

69. A friend of yours has just been raped. She is denying anything happened and looks like she's in shock. Talk to her and convince her to go to the hospital.   *R-he*

70. You suspect that your patient is being physically abused. Try to find out if your suspicions are founded.   *R-he*

Introductions

1. Introduce yourself to your classmate. Tell your classmate where you are from and why you are studying English.   *R-in*

2. Start a conversation and introduce yourself to a stranger at the beach.   *R-in*

3. You and your friend meet your classmate at a café in town. Introduce your friend.   *R-in*

4. Introduce yourself to your new roommate. Find out about your roommate's family.   *R-in*

5. You see someone about your age sitting alone at the bus stop. Introduce yourself and make small talk.   *R-in*

6. You are sitting in the park and see someone you think you've seen before at work. Introduce yourself to this person and find out if she also works at your company.   *R-in*

7. Introduce your lover to your mother.   *R-in*

8. Introduce your date to your father.   *R-in*

9. Introduce your sister to your best friend.   *R-in*

10. Your spouse is meeting you at school and wants to find out what you have been studying and how you are doing in class. Introduce your teacher to your spouse.   *R-in*

11. You have just joined a health club but you don't know anyone there. You are feeling overweight and wondering what you are doing there. All of a sudden a beautiful body approaches you and says "Hi." Introduce yourself.   *R-in*

12. You have decided to join a club in order to meet new people. Introduce yourself and find out about the other members.   *R-in*

13. Introduce someone who doesn't speak English to a friend who only speaks English.   *R-in*

14. You go to a sports event and sit next to someone you don't know. Introduce yourself and talk about the game.   *R-in*

15. Introduce yourself to a new employee at your company who seems very shy.   *R-in*

16. Introduce yourself to your new host family.   *R-in*

17. Your parents are visiting you at your new apartment. You forgot to tell your family that you had a roommate of the opposite sex. Introduce them to your friend.   *R-in*

18. You have just moved into a new apartment. Introduce yourself to your new neighbor.   *R-in*

19. Introduce your child to your date.   *R-in*

20. You are at a party. Introduce yourself to someone you don't know but have been hoping to meet.   *R-in*

21. A friend invited you to someone's party. Introduce yourself to the person giving the party and thank your host for allowing you to attend.   *R-in*

22. You are at a party. You see someone from your class sitting alone. Go over and talk to your classmate about the food.   R-in

23. You are at a dance and make eye contact with someone who you think might be interested in you. Go over and introduce yourself.   *R-in*

24. You meet your ex-spouse at a museum. Introduce your ex to your present spouse.   *R-in*

25. You would like to meet someone you've seen around the neighborhood. Unfortunately, this person speaks only limited English. Introduce yourself and try to communicate.   *R-in*

26. At a café you and your current friend run into someone you used to date. Introduce them.   *R-in*

27. Introduce your child to your date's child.   *R-in*

28. You are the chairperson of the graduation committee. It is graduation day. Introduce the guest speaker.   *R-in*

Invitations

1. Ask a friend to go with you to the movies.   *R-inv*

2. Your classmate has asked you to join him for a drink. Decline the invitation without hurting his feelings.   *R-inv*

3. Ask your classmate to meet you after class so that you can study together.   *R-inv*

4. You see someone sitting alone in the cafeteria. Ask this person if you can sit down.   *R-inv*

5. Ask someone in the class to go out on a date with you.   *R-inv*

6. You are late for an important appointment but you see a classmate whom you really would like to get to know. Tell the classmate that you are in a rush and arrange a meeting later.   *R-inv*

7. You are on a bus going to the fairgrounds. You see a tourist holding an advertisement to the fair. Ask the tourist to join you. *R-inv*

8. There is someone who works at the library whom you would like to get to know better. Invite this person to your home for dinner.   *R-inv*

9. Your friend's parent is visiting from another city. Invite your friend and the parent to join you for dinner. *R-inv*

10. Invite a friend over to your home for a soak in your hot-tub. *R-inv*

11. Someone you don't know very well is inviting you over to his house. You are uncomfortable and a little afraid. What do you say? *R-inv*

12. You received an invitation to a party on Saturday, but you had already made plans for that day. You want to make sure that this friend invites you next time there is a party. Talk to the friend and explain why you cannot attend. *R-inv*

13. Several of your friends are going on a camping trip, but no one has asked you. Talk to one of your friends and try to get yourself invited. *R-inv*

14. Some of your classmates are hiking to a hot springs for a swim. A friend asks you to come along. You want to make sure that they are all bringing bathing suits because you are too embarrassed to go skinny dipping. You don't want your friend to think you are a prude, but you want to find out if they will wear suits. *R-inv*

15. Invite your parent to meet your fiancé's parent. *R-inv*

16. You are invited to a friend's party. You don't know the friend very well, and you are concerned that there will be narcotics there. You want to make friends, but you don't want to be around anything illegal. Thank the friend for inviting you, but decline the invitation. *R-inv*

17. An acquaintance is inviting you to her house to work on a project with her. You have a girlfriend, and you want to make sure your acquaintance knows this beforehand. Talk to her. *R-inv*

18. You received an invitation to a birthday party. At the bottom of the invitation it said R.S.V.P. by a certain date. Unfortunately, you forgot to respond. Now you are embarrassed because the party is tonight and the R.S.V.P. date has passed. Talk to the person who sent you the invitation. *R-inv*

19. You are invited to a wedding, and you would like to bring a few out-of-town guests with you. Ask the person who sent you the invitation if this would be appropriate. *R-inv*

20. You have been invited to your first bachelor party, and you are not sure if you should bring a gift or not. Talk to a friend about what you should do and what to expect at the party. *R-inv*

Jobs (Getting a Job)

1. Ask your teacher if you could use her name for a job reference. *R-gej*

2. Your friend owns a small retail store. Ask him if he could give you a job. *R-gej*

3. You have never had a job before. Ask a friend if looking through the paper is the best way to find job openings.   *R-gej*

4. You have recently graduated from high school and have no idea what to do with your life. You really do not want a job, especially because all your friends are just hanging out. What do you say when one of your parent's friends calls and tells you about a job possibility?   *R-gej*

5. Although you have been trained as a chef, you have been out of work for several months. You are now desperate to get anything and are applying as a dishwasher at a local restaurant. Talk to the owner about the dishwasher position.   *R-gej*

6. You are applying for a position as a file-clerk. You really would like to be the office manager, but there is no opening right now. Tell the head of personnel why you want the file-clerk position.   *R-gej*

7. Your friend has been unemployed for several months. She asks you if there are any openings where you work. Although there are some openings, you are hesitant to tell your friend because you would prefer not to work with her. Talk to her about this.   *R-gej*

8. Your friend has been in jail for the last few months. He was caught in possession of drugs. Now he is applying for a job and needs a recommendation. He asks you if you would recommend him. What do you say?   *R-gej*

9. You go to the Employment Development Office to apply for unemployment. You also need to get a new job. Find out what you have to do to enroll to get some job training.   *R-gej*

10. You've been laid off at least until your company gets a new contract. Go to a temporary employment agency and find out what they can do to help you get employment.   *R-gej*

11. You arrive for a job interview early. While you are waiting, you see your best friend leaving the personnel office. She has just completed her own interview. Talk to her.   *R-gej*

12. As you enter the room for your job interview at an excellent company, you see that the person who will be interviewing you is someone you know but don't like. What do you say?   *R-gej*

13. You just received a phone call telling you to come to an interview tomorrow. Ask your friend what you should wear and how you should act.   *R-gej*

14. You are at an job interview, and the interviewer is asking you some personal questions. Tell the interviewer that you feel uncomfortable with personal questions.   *R-gej*

15. You have been on workers compensation insurance for several years as a result of an accident you had at your last job. You want to plan a good answer for when you are at an interview and the interviewer asks you why you haven't worked for so long. Talk to your friend about what you can say.   *R-gej*

16. Talk to the receptionist of a large office about job opportunities in the company. Ask if you can fill out an application. *R-gej*

17. You are the sales associate at a major department store. A young man approaches you and asks you to help him choose clothes appropriate for interviewing. *R-gej*

18. Your friend asks you to look over her resume before she sends it out. You find many errors. Talk to her about what she needs to do to make it look more professional. *R-gej*

19. You would like to find out more about what it takes to become a medical technician. Go to the local hospital and ask the desk clerk how you can find out about this career. *R-gej*

20. You are at your school's career center. Ask the counselor there to give you some advice on how to find a good job. *R-gej*

21. You are looking for a job as an actor. You have auditioned for several parts, and have been rejected for all of them. Talk to a friend about how you feel and what you can do. *R-gej*

22. After finishing high school, you aren't sure what kind of job you are suited for and what you would enjoy doing. Talk to a friend about this problem and ask for advice. *R-gej*

23. You are looking for a job and have sent out several resumes. So far you have not received any job interviews. Tell a friend that you are feeling really depressed about it. *R-gej*

24. Convince an employer that her company needs your skills. Explain to her that even though you realize her company is not hiring, an exception should be made to hire you. *R-gej*

25. Tell your friend that you want to practice some typical questions so that you are prepared when you interview. *R-gej*

26. Speak to the personnel officer at a company and find out what she would suggest you do to get a job there. *R-gej*

27. You pass a shop that has a sign in the window which says "Creative Talent Needed. Apply Within." Go into the shop and ask to speak to the manager about the job. *R-gej*

28. You are attending a job fair and there is a representative from a company where you would love to work. Go over to the representative and make a good impression. *R-gej*

29. When being interviewed for a job, you lied and told the interviewer that you were experienced on the computer. Actually you have never used a computer and were afraid to tell the truth. You have just been told that you got the job. Talk to your friend about your problem. *R-gej*

30. Your friend is having trouble getting a job. Tell him he needs to have a cleaner appearance and to update his wardrobe. *R-gej*

31. You are always very nervous when you have an interview for a job. Your friend just got a good job, and you want to find out what she did right. Ask your friend for some pointers. *R-gej*

32. You have made several appointments to meet with the executive director of a film company for a job. Each time you have brought your portfolio and your resume, and each time the receptionist has told you the director was too busy to see you. Convince the secretary that the executive director must see you today.   *R-gej*

23. Your best friend is out of work and needs to get a job immediately. The problem is that he doesn't have any confidence when he goes for an interview – he gets very nervous. He knows he was fired from his last job, and that it was his fault for covering for a dishonest friend. Help him prepare for his next interview.   *R-gej*

Jobs (On the Job)

1. A co-worker is constantly making sexual comments in your presence. Tell the co-worker that this is disturbing to you.   *R-oj*

2. Your boss seems to be interested in dating you. Talk to your boss about this.   *R-oj*

3. One of your co-workers is making personal calls at work. Tell the co-worker that this is distracting to you.   *R-oj*

4. Ask your employer if the company will pay for a course that you would like to take. Explain how taking this course will benefit your job.   *R-oj*

5. Today is your first day on the job. Talk to the person in charge of benefits about what kinds of programs are available to you.   *R-oj*

6. Talk to your manager. Ask for a raise.   *R-oj*

7. Talk to your boss. Tell her that you feel you deserve a promotion.   *R-oj*

8. Tell your employer that someone is stealing money from the company.   *R-oj*

9. You must fire one of your workers because he has not been doing the job well. Ask the worker to come into your office.   *R-oj*

10. Someone who works at the company asks you if she can get her spouse a job at the company too. You are the chief of personnel. Discuss the possibilities with her.   *R-oj*

11. One of your co-workers is constantly talking to you and you find it difficult to perform your duties. Tell him this.   *R-oj*

12. A co-worker who works at the desk next to you is constantly on the telephone. Complain to the supervisor about this.   *R-oj*

13. Explain to your boss that the reason you haven't been able to get much work done lately is because you are having troubles at home.   *R-oj*

14. You are a contractor and someone has called you to do some remodeling on a house. Talk to this person about the price and the kind of work you would be doing.   *R-oj*

15. Your boss blames you for an accident which occurred at your company. You did not cause the accident. Speak to your employer about this.   *R-oj*

16. Your boss is constantly pressuring you to work overtime. You need to get home to your family. Explain this to your boss.   *R-oj*

17. Tell one of your employees she has been taking too long on breaks and for lunch.   *R-oj*

18. Ask one of your employees why he is always late.   *R-oj*

19. Explain to a new employee what her duties will be.   *R-oj*

20. You have noticed that one of your co-workers is drinking alcohol during lunch and sometimes on the job. Talk to the worker about your concerns.   *R-oj*

21. Tell your boss that someone you are working with is using illegal drugs while on the job.   *R-oj*

22. Ask a co-worker (who is from another country) about job opportunities in his country.   *R-oj*

23. You feel that your employer is unjustly picking on you. Talk to her about this.   *R-oj*

24. Your boss calls you to her office and asks you to take a voluntary pay cut.   *R-oj*

25. Your boss calls you to his office to tell you that new technology has replaced your job and you are being laid off.   *R-oj*

26. Tell your employer that you want to quit the company because you have found a better job with higher pay somewhere else. *R-oj*

27. You would like to start your own business. Talk to a friend who owns his own business to find out what you need to do.   *R-oj*

28. You are thinking about starting your own business. Talk to the bank manager about the possibility of taking out a loan.   *R-oj*

29. You want to start a business but you need capital. Talk to your friend about her becoming a partner and investing in the company.   *R-oj*

Parent-Child Interactions

1. Your child is having problems at school and you were just called in to talk to your child's teacher. Ask your child to explain what's going on at school.   *R-pci*

2. Your child is having a lot of trouble with homework. Talk to your child and find out what the problem is.   *R-pci*

3. Another student in your class has been taking your lunch money. Although you don't want to "squeal," tell your parents.   *R-pci*

4. You do not want to go to school because several students tease you and threaten to beat you up. Tell your parents and ask what to do about the "bullies".   *R-pci*

5. Other children make fun of you because your family does not have much money. You are embarrassed. Tell one of your parents about it.   *R-pci*

6. You have trouble seeing the work on the blackboard at school, but are embarrassed to tell your teacher. Tell your parent.   *R-pci*

7. The teacher has told you that your child is cheating at school. Talk to your child.   *R-pci*

8. Your child is always blaming other children when she is the one at fault. Talk to your child about accepting the responsibility and consequences of her own actions.   *R-pci*

9. Your child is six years old and is always playing with an imaginary friend. You want to be sure your child understands the difference between reality and fantasy. Talk to him.   *R-pci*

10. Your child has trouble concentrating and focusing in school and at home. Find out what the problem is and what you can do.   *R-pci*

11. Your parents are always giving you a hard time about your friends and saying you hang with the wrong crowd. Tell your parents that you know what you are doing and to leave you and your friends alone.   *R-pci*

12. When you were cleaning your son's room you discovered some drug paraphernalia. Discuss this with your son.   *R-pci*

13. Tell one of your parents that your girlfriend is pregnant and it may be your baby.   *R-pci*

14. Your daughter is a freshman at college and wants to go away for the weekend with friends. She asks you for permission. Talk about your concerns.   *R-pci*

15. Your parent thinks it is time for you to move out of the house and live on your own. Unfortunately, you enjoy living at home and not paying rent. Discuss this.   *R-pci*

16. Your mother wants you to meet someone whom she says would be perfect for you. How can you get out of meeting this person without hurting your mom's feelings? Talk to her.   *R-pci*

17. Tell your parents that you have decided to marry someone who is 20 years your senior.   *R-pci*

18. Your teen-ager just got a driver's license and wants to borrow the family car. What do you say?   *R-pci*

19. A rule of the house is that your teen-ager cannot stay out after 10 o'clock on a weekday. Your seventeen-year old wants you to make an exception. What do you say? Discuss this.   *R-pci*

20. You are fifteen years old. Ask your parents for permission to get married.   *R-pci*

21. You have just turned eighteen and want to get married. Ask your mother to give you her blessing.   *R-pci*

22. You are sixteen years old and you want to be an actor. Your parent wants you to take over the family business. Talk to your parent about what you want to do with your life.   *R-pci*

23. You want to quit school and start work, but your mother feels it is important to finish high school. Discuss the options.   *R-pci*

24. Your father wants you to go to college but you feel you are just not smart enough. You do not want to go. Talk about this and explain how you feel and why. *R-pci*

25. Your son has excellent grades and wants to go to college. Unfortunately, you feel that you do not have the finances for him to do this. Discuss this.   *R-pci*

26. Tell your mother or father that you are pregnant.   *R-pci*

27. Tell your fifteen-year old daughter that you are going to have another baby.   *R-pci*

28. You find out that your son took the car without permission. Talk about this.   *R-pci*

29. Tell your parents that you smashed the family car.   *R-pci*

30. Ask your parent to lend you some money to buy a car. *R-pci*

31. Complain to your best friend about your parents.   *R-pci*

32. You are sixteen and you feel you should be able to go out on dates, but your parents feel you are still too young. Discuss this.   *R-pci*

33. Your son has graduated from high school and now just sits around the house. Ask him to look for a job and help out with the rent.   *R-pci*

34. Explain to your seven-year-old son that he is adopted.   *R-pci*

35. Tell your child that you are gay.   *R-pci*

36. Ask your child to help with the housework.   *R-pci*

37. Tell your child that you do not like the "friends" she brings to the house.   *R-pci*

38. Your child has shaved her head and is piercing different body parts. Talk to her about this.   *R-pci*

39. Your child was suspended from school because he was carrying a weapon. He doesn't seem to care, and you are worried about him.   *R-pci*

40. Lately your child has begun to get very angry and you are worried that this is destructive. Talk to your child.   *R-pci*

41. You would like to go with your child to counseling. Convince your child to go with you. *R-pci*

42. You have started drinking alcohol with your friends at school. Your parent confronts you with proof that you've been drinking. What can you say?   *R-pci*

43. Tell your parents that you have tested positive for a sexually transmitted disease.   *R-pci*

44. Tell your child that you are HIV positive.   *R-pci*

45. Explain to your child that you and your spouse are getting divorced.   *R-pci*

46. Tell your child that you are considering getting married again. Ask for your child's opinion. *R-pci*

47. Tell your parent that you are hurt and upset because of all the verbal abuse in the house. Threaten to run away from home unless it stops.   *R-pci*

48. You are furious because you hit your child and your child had the nerve to strike you back. Discuss your anger with your child. *R-pci*

49. You think one of your parents is making sexual advances towards you, but you are not completely sure. You think maybe you are imagining this. Talk to your other parent. *R-pci*

50. One of your parent's friends has been coming into your room late at night after your parent is asleep. You were told by that person that this is a secret friendship and you are not to tell anyone or you will be sorry. Even though you are afraid, tell your parent about this. *R-pci*

51. Your child is thirteen years old and you have never talked about sex. Sit down and begin a conversation about sex with your child. *R-pci*

52. After your grandmother dies, your parents decided to invite your grandfather to live with you and your family. Nobody asked your opinion. Tell your parents how you feel. *R-pci*

53. You feel that your sibling gets better treatment from your parent. Tell your parent this. *R-pci*

54. One of your parents seems tired and unhappy. Ask what the matter is. *R-pci*

55. Your parents want to move, but you do not want to leave your friends. Talk about this. *R-pci*

56. You do not want to do the chores your parents have told you to do. Tell them this. *R-pci*

57. The family needs to stop spending so much money because you are finding it difficult to pay all the bills. Talk to your child about limiting spending. *R-pci*

58. Your parents do not give you an allowance and you never have any money to buy what you want. All your friends have their own money. Ask your parents to give you an allowance. *R-pci*

59. Your child constantly watches rock videos in his room with the door shut. You are worried that your child doesn't get out of the house and get any exercise. Talk to your child about this. *R-pci*

60. You are concerned because your child is losing a lot of weight very quickly. You think she may be anorexic because you never see her eat. Talk to her. *R-pci*

61. Tell your parent that you did not get on the school's swim team. *R-pci*

62. Tell your parent that you got the lead in the school play. *R-pci*

63. Tell your parent that her drinking is embarrassing to you. *R-pci*

64. Ask your parent not to interrogate your dates. *R-pci*

65. You think your child is not going to the school prom because he doesn't know how to dance. Offer to teach him. *R-pci*

66. Ask your parent to allow you to take a driving class. *R-pci*

67. You think your child may be dyslexic. Talk to your child about problems at school. *R-pci*

68. You have not been able to pay attention at home or in school. Ask your parents for help. *R-pci*

69. Tell your parents that you want to move out of the house.   *R-pci*

70. Explain to your child that your spouse has left the house and may not return.   *R-pci*

71. Your spouse is physically abusive to you and your child. Although you are frightened for your own safety, you know you need to take your child and leave your spouse. Talk to your child about your escape.   *R-pci*

72. Your parents are divorced, and your father has custody. Tell your father that you do not want to visit your mother anymore.   *R-pci*

73. One of your parents has been in a drug treatment program. You would like to tell your parent that you are very proud that she has overcome her problem and that you want to help.   *R-pci*

74. Your parents are becoming very old and want to live with you and your family. What do you say?   *R-pci*

75. Your elderly parent does not want to talk about death, but you want to find out if there is a will. You would be more comfortable knowing where the important papers are and what to do in the event of your parent's death.   *R-pci*

76. An older sibling refuses to help care for your aging parent. Your parent depends totally on you, and you need a life of your own. Talk to your parent about this problem.   *R-pci*

77. Your parent with Alzheimer's disease is becoming more and more difficult to take care of. Presently both your parents live together, but the parent who is the caregiver feels overwhelmed. Talk to your caregiver parent about options available.   *R-pci*

78. Your parent does not drive and depends on you for trips to the doctor, shopping, etc. You have a family of your own and small children to care for. Tell your parent that you need to set limits.   *R-pci*

79. Your three-year-old does not want to go to day care anymore because, according to your child, there aren't enough toys and your child has no one to play with. You know this is not true, but your child needs to be comforted. Talk to your child about going to day care.   *R-pci*

80. Your teen-ager has started to behave rudely to you and your friends. In addition, she refuses to do any chores or to obey curfew. When you ask what's going on, she tells you to mind your own business. Try to talk with her.   *R-pci*

81. Your child's school counselor has told you that your child is fighting with the other children. Talk to your child about the problem.   *R-pci*

82. Your child was in a fight with another child at school. Your child told you that he did nothing and that the other child started it. Talk to your son about what to do in this situation. *R-pci*

Restaurants

1. Tell your waiter that the drink she has just served you has no alcohol in it. Ask her to take it back and bring you another. *R-re*

2. You are a waiter in a busy restaurant. One of your customers keeps calling you over and changing his order. *R-re*

3. You are seated at a table in a very elegant restaurant. The person sitting at the next table is eating noisily and disturbing you. Ask the restaurant host if you can change to another table. *R-re*

4. You are eating dinner alone. At the next table someone is winking at you and this bothers you. Ask the person to stop. *R-re*

5. You have just finished your meal at the restaurant. Your waiter brings the check, but you realize you don't have enough money with you to pay the bill. *R-re*

6. Your waiter brought you the wrong order and you are in a hurry. Demand the correct order. *R-re*

7. You ordered Steak Tartare not knowing that this is uncooked meat. When you see what it is, you know you cannot eat it. Although you do not want to appear ignorant, you must talk to the waiter. What do you say? *R-re*

8. You are in an airplane and the flight attendant brings you your meal. It has meat in it, and you are a strict vegetarian. Explain why you can't eat it. *R-re*

9. One of your customers wants to change her order after you have brought it to her. Explain to the customer that the order cannot be changed; it is restaurant policy. *R-re*

10. Your waiter trips and drops a full tray in your lap. You are covered with food. Ask if the waiter or restaurant will pay the bill for dry cleaning your clothes. *R-re*

11. It is your first day on the job, and you are the only waiter at a crowded restaurant. Several of your customers are becoming impatient and calling you at the same time. You are nervous and feel like running away. Talk to one particularly irritating customer. *R-re*

12. Your friend takes you to a Japanese restaurant for your birthday and orders sushi for you both. You know you will not like raw fish, but your friend insists you try it. What do you say? *R-re*

13. You ordered your steak medium rare, but your waiter brought you one that is black. Tell the waiter to take it back. *R-re*

14. You are walking to your table. Accidentally, you hit someone's arm and that person spills hot coffee all over himself. *R-re*

15. Tell the waiter that there are smokers in the non-smoking section of the restaurant. *R-re*

16. You are trying a restaurant for the first time. When you taste your order, it is inedible. Tell the waiter. *R-re*

17. You are waiting for a table at a restaurant. The host is not paying attention to your group and is letting others in ahead of you. Tell the host that you have been waiting for a long time and that it is your turn. *R-re*

18. You are in a very elegant restaurant with a date that you want to impress. The waiter brings you the bill, and you see that you have been overcharged. What do you do? *R-re*

19. You were supposed to receive an important telephone call at this restaurant a half-hour ago. Find out from the waiter if anyone has left a message for you. *R-re*

20. You are a waiter at a restaurant. One of the customers is being rude to you. What do you say? *R-re*

21. You are sitting at the bar in a restaurant. You leave your jacket on the back of the chair and go to the restroom. When you return, someone is sitting in your seat. Ask the person to give you your seat. *R-re*

22. You are the waiter at a very fashionable restaurant. One of your customers is making sexual advances towards you. Tell this person to stop this behavior and let you work. *R-re*

23. You are on your first date with someone you really like. After finishing dinner, your date puts down half the cost of the two dinners. You didn't bring enough money to pay for your meal because you thought the person who does the inviting pays. Explain this to your date. *R-re*

24. Your friend who is visiting you from another country has bought you dinner and has left no tip for the waiter. You do not know if your friend is unaware of this custom or intentionally wants to "stiff" the waiter for a reason. Talk to your friend. *R-re*

25. You are visiting another city and have eaten a very inexpensive meal at a small restaurant. You left no tip not because the service was poor, but because you had little change left. The waiter says something rude to you as you leave the restaurant. *R-re*

26. The service at the restaurant you and your friend have just eaten at is very poor. You do not want to leave a tip. Talk about this with your friend. *R-re*

27. Find out from a tourist information center where the best inexpensive restaurants are in the area. *R-re*

28. You and a friend are seated at a restaurant and you realize that you are the only customers. You feel uncomfortable and want to leave. What do you do? *R-re*

29. You are with a friend who is eating and talking at the same time. You find this embarrassing and disgusting. Ask your friend to not talk with a mouth full of food. *R-re*

30. You are in the restroom at a restaurant. While you are using the facilities, you hear someone talking to someone else in the restroom about your date. Find out how this person knows your date. *R-re*

31. Your friend has just arrived in this country and you are taking him out to eat. When the soup arrives, he sips from the bowl rather than using the spoon offered. Try to explain politely that customs are different here and that using a spoon is more appropriate.   *R-re*

32. You are supposed to meet an important client at a posh restaurant. Unfortunately, you did not know that there is a dress code. When you arrive at the restaurant, the doorkeeper refuses to admit you because you are not appropriately dressed. Convince the doorkeeper to let you in. *R-re*

Roommates

1. Your roommate is playing the CD player so loud that you can't get to sleep. Ask your roommate to turn down the volume and have some consideration for you. *R-ro*

2. Your roommate gets up in the middle of the night, cooks a big meal, and leaves all the dishes until the morning. You always wake up to a real mess in the kitchen. Talk to your roommate about this.   *R-ro*

3. Your roommate always brings her friends into your apartment. One couple is always very loud. They bring their own music, which you don't enjoy. And they leave the apartment a mess. You don't like these friends. Discuss this problem with your roommate.   *R-ro*

4. Although you bought the TV, your roommate watches it most of the time. For some reason, the TV has stopped working. Tell your roommate to pay for the repair.   *R-ro*

5. You are sure that you left your wallet on the kitchen table in your apartment. When you get home, it is gone. Ask your roommate about it.   *R-ro*

6. Your roommate is not very neat and you are tired of picking up after her. Discuss the problem with your roommate.   *R-ro*

7. Your roommate's girlfriend is spending a lot of time at your apartment. Tell your roommate that this bothers you.   *R-ro*

8. You feel you and your roommate are no longer get along. Ask your roommate to move out.   *R-ro*

9. Even though you and your roommate agreed to clean the house on alternate weekends, you are the one doing all the house cleaning. Remind your roommate about your agreement.   *R-ro*

10. You would like your roommate to move out of the apartment because you want your lover to move in. Tell your roommate your plans.   *R-ro*

11. Your mother called last night and your roommate was rude to her. Your mother was very upset when you spoke to her. Talk to your roommate about this.   *R-ro*

12. Your roommate always leaves the lights on in your apartment. Explain that your electric bills are getting too high.   *R-ro*

13. Your roommate is constantly talking on the telephone. You need to make an important call and you have been waiting for your roommate to hang up for almost an hour. Tell your roommate to get off the phone or you will disconnect it.   *R-ro*

14. Your roommate keeps some recreational drugs in her room. Explain to her that it is dangerous and illegal for both of you.   *R-ro*

15. You cook dinner and your roommate washes the dishes every night. Unfortunately, the dishes are not always completely clean and now you have an ant problem in your cupboards. Tell your roommate about this without getting angry.   *R-ro*

16. Tell your roommate that you have found another apartment for yourself and you want to move out.   *R-ro*

17. Ask your roommate to stop eating all your food in the refrigerator.   *R-ro*

18. Your roommate has a pet that you are constantly cleaning up after. Tell your friend to either start caring for the pet or get rid of it.   *R-ro*

19. Your roommate thinks that you should pay more rent because your room is larger. You feel that you are both sharing the house, so the rent should really be split equally. Discuss this.   *R-ro*

20. Your roommate's friend wants to come and spend a few weeks in your apartment. You feel that the house will be too crowded and you want to have privacy. Tell your roommate that you do not like this idea.   *R-ro*

21. You and your roommate want to have a party. Plan it together and share the expenses.   *R-ro*

22. You need a roommate, and you have placed an ad in the local paper. Someone comes to your door in response to the ad. Talk to this person and see if you are compatible.   *R-ro*

23. Convince a friend that the two of you should get an apartment together.   *R-ro*

24. Your friend asks you to be his roommate, but you'd prefer to live alone. Tell him this without hurting his feelings.   *R-ro*

25. You and a friend are planning to be roommates. Discuss what you will need to get to furnish your new apartment.   *R-ro*

26. Your friend is excited about moving in with you. Your friend thinks you are going to put your stereo and TV in the living room to share, when actually you want these things in your room. Explain to your friend that you would like to straighten these things out before you move in together.   *R-ro*

27. You are planning to move into an apartment with a platonic friend of the opposite sex. Your friend is having difficulties explaining this to her parents. Talk to her about how you can help.   *R-ro*

28. Your roommate has a different person sleeping over every night. You do not like having strange people in the house. Furthermore, you are worried about your roommate and the threat of AIDS. Talk to your friend about your concerns.   *R-ro*

29. Last night you heard a lot of noise from your roommate's room. You know your roommate has a bad temper. This morning you see your roommate's guest with a bruised eye and a swollen lip.Talk to the guest about what happened.   *R-ro*

30. A stray cat has been coming to your door for the last few weeks begging for food. You have been feeding it, and you would like to take the cat in. However, your apartment does not allow pets. Talk to your roommate about what you should do.   *R-ro*

31. Tell your roommate that you have tested HIV positive.   *R-ro*

32. Tell your roommate that you have fallen in love with him and ask if you should move out.   *R-ro*

33. Your roommate smokes cigarettes in the house. She's a heavy smoker, and you are concerned about second-hand smoke and how it will affect you. Talk to your roommate.   *R-ro*

34. Your roommate has two children and is divorced. The children come over every other weekend. When they visit, they play all over the apartment and create a mess which you have to take care of. Talk to your roommate about this.   *R-ro*

35. Your roommate has lost a lot of weight, and you suspect that she may be anorexic. Talk to her about her health.   *R-ro*

36. You think that your roommate has been "borrowing" some of your things without permission. Talk to your roommate.   *R-ro*

37. It is three o'clock in the morning. Your roommate has forgotten her house keys again. When she rings the doorbell and bangs on the door, tell her to find somewhere else to sleep and to leave you alone.   *R-ro*

38. Tell your roommate that you have lost the keys to the house and that all the locks need to be changed again.   *R-ro*

School

(Student's View)

1. You want to enroll in school. Ask the receptionist for some information and an entrance application.   *R-ssv*

2. Ask your school counselor what schools he thinks you should apply to for graduate work.   *R-ssv*

3. Your friend has been accepted to the school of her choice. You were rejected. Tell her how you feel.   *R-ssv*

4. Tell your teacher that you want to apply to a university in the US and ask if she would write you a recommendation.   *R-ssv*

5. Even though your grades are not very good, you think you want to go to university. Talk to your school counselor about the possibilities open to you.   *R-ssv*

6. You feel your teacher is constantly picking on you. Confront her about this.   *R-ssv*

7. You do not feel that you received a fair grade on a paper. You worked hard and still got the lowest grade in the class. Talk to your teacher.   *R-ssv*

8. Your entire class feels that the teacher is boring. Your teacher asks you to stay after class to talk about why you're falling asleep during class. Tell the teacher how you feel.   *R-ssv*

9. You feel that your teacher and classmates are constantly fooling around and you are not getting the education you paid for. Talk to your teacher about this. *R-ssv*

10. Several of your classmates carry weapons to school. You are frightened that something terrible is going to happen. Talk to your teacher.   *R-ssv*

11. You know of several people who are selling illegal drugs on campus. You don't like this, but you do not want to get into any trouble. Talk to a friend about what you can do.   *R-ssv*

12. Several students in your class tease you and you are very uncomfortable in class. Talk to your school counselor.   *R-ssv*

13. You would like to go to college, but your family needs you to work. Talk to your school counselor about your options. *R-ssv*

14. Your teacher is talking about sex and AIDS in class. Talk to a friend about how uncomfortable you feel.   *R-ssv*

15. You have decided not to attend school today. After school, your teacher sees you at the mall and comes over to talk to you. What do you say?   *R-ssv*

16. Your parents want you to finish high school, but you really think school is a waste of time for you. Talk about this.   *R-ssv*

17. You want to do better in school, but you just can't seem to concentrate and get your work done. Talk to your teacher.   *R-ssv*

18. Almost everyday many of your friends drink alcohol in school at lunch time. Talk to one of your friends about this. *R-ssv*

19. You would like to go to another country on a school exchange program. Your parent doesn't think you are mature enough to do this. Talk about it.   *R-ssv*

20. Your parents are constantly fighting with each other. You would like to go to an out-of-town college just to get away from them. Talk to your school counselor about this.   *R-ssv*

21. You just took a very difficult exam. You feel the exam was unfair because there were several things on it that your class had not studied. Talk to your teacher after class.   *R-ssv*

22. You think your class is too difficult. Your teacher feels you just need to work harder. Discuss this with your teacher.   *R-ssv*

23. Tell your teacher that you don't understand what's going on in class. You are working hard, but getting more and more confused. Ask your teacher to help you after school.   *R-ssv*

24. Tell your teacher that you want to quit school.   *R-ssv*

25. Tell your favorite teacher that you appreciate all her efforts and that she is your role model.   *R-ssv*

School

(Teacher's view)

1. You are a teacher with a difficult class. Talk to one of the troublemakers about her behavior. *R-stv*

2. One of your students comes to class after being absent for several days. You notice that his face is badly bruised. Talk to him about it.   *R-stv*

3. You suspect that one of your students has cheated on an exam. Talk to her.   *R-stv*

4. Talk to a student who is always late for class. Explain that this behavior is unacceptable. *R-stv*

5. Talk to a co-worker about different ways to motivate your class.   *R-stv*

6. One of your students who works at night is always falling asleep in class. Talk to him about this.   *R-stv*

7. You are losing patience with a class of yours that is just not learning. Talk to a friend about what you can do.   *R-stv*

8. You are starting to get burned out on teaching, but you have never worked at any other occupation. Talk to a friend about whether you should continue teaching or try something else.   *R-stv*

9. You are asked to come into your supervisor's office because one of your students has complained about you. Talk to your supervisor about this.   *R-stv*

10. A group of students in your class seem to dislike another student. You have overheard a threat and are beginning to feel afraid for the student's safety. Talk to the student and find out what the problem is.   *R-stv*

11. Tell your supervisor that you feel you need to take a leave of absence.   *R-stv*

12. Talk to a student who never does her homework. Ask her what is troubling her.   *R-stv*

13. You suspect one of your students is pregnant. Talk to her.   *R-stv*

14. Talk to your brightest student about his future goals.   *R-stv*

15. Ask one of your weakest students about his goals.   *R-stv*

16. Talk to one of your students about why she is always failing your exams.   *R-stv*

17. You suspect one of your students is selling illegal drugs. Call the student into your office.   *R-stv*

18. Talk to one of your students who is disruptive about his poor attitude. *R-stv*

19. Talk to the teacher who taught your class last semester. Find out what problems she had with the class. *R-stv*

20. You have an important appointment away from school tomorrow. Ask one of your fellow teachers if he can substitute for you while you are gone. Tell him about your class and the work he will need to cover. *R-stv*

Spouses

1. Discuss your financial difficulties with your spouse. Although your spouse doesn't want to work outside the home, explain that you will both need to have jobs in order to get out of debt. *R-sp*

2. Tell your spouse that you feel you are doing all the domestic chores and that you want to share the housework equally. *R-sp*

3. You and your spouse live with the children from your first marriage. The children don't like your spouse, and your spouse is having a difficult time disciplining them. Tell your spouse that this is straining your marriage, and together figure out what to do. *R-sp*

4. Tell your spouse that you are not in love anymore. *R-sp*

5. After twenty years, you are still in love with your spouse. Talk about renewing your vows. *R-sp*

6. Tell your spouse that you are in love with someone else. *R-sp*

7. Your spouse has been home taking care of the children but now wants to return to work. Discuss how you feel about putting the children in day care. *R-sp*

8. Your spouse wants to ask grandma to watch the children during the day when your spouse returns to work. You feel grandma is not competent enough to watch young children, and besides you feel it would be taking advantage of her. Discuss the alternatives with your spouse. *R-sp*

9. You and your spouse both work all day, and your two children are in day care. The center has a good reputation, but your children are not happy there. Tell your spouse that one of you should stop working and stay at home during the day. *R-sp*

10. You want to have a child. Your spouse doesn't. Don't argue, but discuss this quietly. *R-sp*

11. You want to adopt a child, but your spouse thinks you should just keep trying to have one of your own. Talk to your spouse about your feelings. *R-sp*

12. Tell your spouse that you have just heard that you have a sexually transmitted disease. *R-sp*

13. Tell your spouse that you think it is time that you moved to another city. *R-sp*

14. Tell your spouse that you do not want your mother-in-law interfering with your lives anymore. *R-sp*

15. Tell your spouse that you want your meals prepared and ready when you come home from work. *R-sp*

16. Tell your husband that you think you are pregnant. *R-sp*

17. Tell your spouse that you would like to take a vacation alone. *R-sp*

18. Tell your spouse that you would like to go out more often. *R-sp*

19. Tell your spouse that you think she should find a new, higher paying job. *R-sp*

20. Tell your spouse that you think he spends too much money on clothes. *R-sp*

21. Ask your spouse to spend some quality time with you. *R-sp*

22. You always had a pet when you were growing up, but your spouse did not. Convince your spouse that it is time to get a dog for your children. *R-sp*

23. Your husband wants to stay home and watch the children, and he feels that you should go out and work. Discuss this arrangement. *R-sp*

24. Your husband wants you to stay home, cook, and take care of the house, but you want to get a job. Discuss this. *R-sp*

25. Your wife is pregnant. She is frightened because she feels the two of you do not have enough financial security to have a baby right now. Talk to her. *R-sp*

26. Tell your spouse she snores at night and you cannot get to sleep. *R-sp*

27. You are pregnant. Your husband really wants to have a little boy. You are very worried that if you have a girl, he will be displeased. Discuss this. *R-sp*

28. You are pregnant, and you want your husband to go with you to natural childbirth classes. He doesn't want to go. Convince him to be your coach. *R-sp*

29. You and your wife have been having a lot of problems lately. Your wife wants to leave you and live with her mother. You do not want her to go. You don't like to beg, but you would prefer that she stay so you two can work things out together. *R-sp*

30. You and your husband have just returned from your honeymoon and you find out you're pregnant. It is a bad time for the two of you because you are not financially settled. You were hoping to be able to work because your husband's job is not very secure. Talk to your husband about what to do. *R-sp*

31. You have been on fertility pills and now you are finally pregnant. Tell your husband that your doctor says you will be having quadruplets. *R-sp*

32. You are very pregnant. You and your husband are in the United States visiting relatives. Your husband wants you to have your baby back in your native country. Tell him you would like to have the baby in the US so that it will have American citizenship. *R-sp*

33. Your wife is about to have a baby. She wants to have a midwife deliver the baby at home. Convince her that it will be better if she goes to a hospital.　*R-sp*

34. Tell your spouse that you need a night out and you are going out with your single friends.　*R-sp*

35. Tell your spouse that you should hire a babysitter and have a romantic date together.　*R-sp*

36. Confess to your mate that several years ago you committed adultery.　*R-sp*

37. Decide on a name for your soon-to-be-born child.　*R-sp*

38. Your spouse is very jealous of the people you work with. Talk about it.　*R-sp*

39. You forgot your anniversary. Apologize to your spouse and try to celebrate.　*R-sp*

40. Your wife is having a baby. You have been waiting for six hours. Talk to another expectant father at the hospital.　*R-sp*

41. You would like to buy your spouse a birthday present, but you really don't know what to get. Find out what your spouse wants without letting your spouse know what you are doing.　*R-sp*

42. Tell your partner why you feel you have an "ideal" marriage.　*R-sp*

43. Tell your partner that you want a divorce.　*R-sp*

44. Your spouse is very possessive and does not want you to see or talk to your friends. You are worried that your spouse might hurt you if you don't obey. Try to reason with your spouse.　*R-sp*

45. You and your spouse are of different religions. You want to have children someday. Discuss what religion you want your children to be.　*R-sp*

46. You would like to adopt a baby. You do not care about the baby's color or ethnicity. Your spouse does not believe in interracial adoption. Talk to your spouse about this.　*R-sp*

47. You are twenty weeks pregnant and have an amniocentesis. The results confirm that your baby has Down's Syndrome. Talk to your spouse about what you will do.　*R-sp*

48. You are in your early forties and would like to try to have a child. The doctor has told you if you want to have children, you can't wait much longer. Talk to your spouse and find out if this is the right time.　*R-sp*

49. You do not believe in spanking your children, but your spouse does. Discuss alternative ways to punish your children.　*R-sp*

50. You are the stepparent of two adolescents. These children are rude to you and do not make you feel like you are part of the family. Talk to your spouse about this.　*R-sp*

51. Your spouse's father, who lived in another state, has just passed away. Console your spouse.　*R-sp*

52. Discuss with your spouse how to explain to your child that his grandfather has died.　*R-sp*

53. Discuss the idea of you and your spouse becoming foster parents.　*R-sp*

54. You and your wife were separated for six months. During that time you were dating other people. Now you are back with your wife, but have discovered that one of the women you were dating is pregnant with your child. Talk to your wife. *R-sp*

55. Talk to your spouse about being a surrogate parent for a couple who cannot have children of their own. *R-sp*

56. You feel that you and your spouse are more like roommates than lovers. Talk to your spouse about the lack of intimacy in your relationship. *R-sp*

57. Ask your spouse what you can do to be more romantic. *R-sp*

58. Talk with your spouse about whether your children are old enough to come home from school and take care of themselves until you arrive home from work. *R-sp*

59. Having had a very troubled childhood, your partner is concerned about being a good parent. Talk to your partner about this issue. *R-sp*

60. Tell your partner that the two of you need to sneak away and do something spontaneous right now. *R-sp*

61. While you were shopping with your two-year-old twins, someone stopped you and asked if you were the mother or the grandmother. Ask your husband if you really look like you're getting old. *R-sp*

62. You have been separated from your spouse for a short time and you had been hoping to get back together. You have just learned that your spouse has a new lover, someone who has been your friend for years. Go to your spouse and find out what's going on. *R-sp*

Telephone

1. A friend of yours thinks you should meet more people. She gave you the phone number of one of her friends. Telephone this person. Invite the person to meet you at a café. *R-te*

2. You miss your friend because you are in different countries right now. Call your friend and share your feelings. *R-te*

3. Call your parent in your native country. Explain what you have been doing. *R-te*

4. Call your parent and ask to borrow some money. *R-te*

5. Call the telephone company and tell them that something is wrong with your phone. *R-te*

6. You have just moved to another state and you are miserable. Call your one of your parents and talk about whether you should return home. *R-te*

7. You smell smoke in your house. Call the fire department. *R-te*

8. Call the police and tell them you have been robbed. *R-te*

9. You have a terrible toothache. When you call your dentist to make an appointment, you are told the dentist is very busy. Explain that this is an emergency. *R-te*

10. You are awakened in the middle of the night by the sound of your bedroom window opening. Call 911 and tell them to come to your home immediately. *R-te*

11. Telephone your friend. Find out why your friend has not called you recently. *R-te*

12. You are invited to a party, but have made previous plans. Call your friend and explain that you are very sorry but can't attend the celebration. *R-te*

13. Call a classmate to find out what went on today in class. Tell your friend that you were sick and ask your friend to explain the homework to you. *R-te*

14. You have just found out that a good friend of yours in another country just had a baby. Call your friend to congratulate the happy parent. *R-te*

15. Your sibling has just become engaged. When you call to offer your congratulations, you find out your sibling is marrying someone you used to date. *R-te*

16. You have been invited to a good friend's wedding in another state. You will be unable to attend. Call your friend and explain that you cannot be there. *R-te*

17. This is your first holiday without your family. Call them and wish them a happy holiday. *R-te*

18. You just got a letter from your fiancé who has been in another country. The letter says that you need to call the wedding off because things have changed. You are shocked. Call your fiancé and discuss this. *R-te*

19. Call your best friend in another part of the country and ask if your friend can come visit you. *R-te*

20. You want to buy tickets to a concert. Call the telephone number of the theater and find out more information. *R-te*

21. You are supposed to meet a friend of yours for dinner but will be unable to make it. Call the restaurant and ask if it is possible for you to leave a message for your friend with the restaurant. *R-te*

22. Call an old friend. You haven't been in touch with your friend for years. Find out if your friend is married and what your friend has been doing. *R-te*

23. You are looking for a new place to live. Call and inquire about an apartment you saw in the newspaper. *R-te*

24. You are looking for a job. Call about one you saw listed in the paper. *R-te*

25. You are looking for a used car at a reasonable price. You see one offered in a box ad in the local paper. Call the number given in the ad. *R-te*

26. Call the cable TV company and ask them how to get cable installed in your house.   *R-te*

27. You want to stay in the US to study, but your family wants you to come home soon. Telephone your parents and ask if you can remain longer.   *R-te*

28. Tell the operator that you are having trouble placing a call and ask the operator to connect you.   *R-te*

29. Tell the phone company that you think they made an error on your last bill.   *R-te*

30. Make a collect call to a friend from a public telephone booth.   *R-te*

31. You telephone your friend but the person who answers is very difficult to understand.   *R-te*

32. Call about an ad you found in the newspaper. It said, "Make new friends and meet hundreds of new people."   *R-te*

33. Your toilet has backed up and the water is pouring all over the floor. Call a plumber.   *R-te*

34. Call the person for whom you babysit and explain that you are not feeling well enough to come over today.   *R-te*

35. Someone in your best friend's family has just died. Telephone your friend and say that you are very sorry to hear it.   *R-te*

36. The roofers have put a new roof on your house, and after the first big rain, it is leaking. Call the roofers and demand that they come to your home right away.   *R-te*

37. You hired someone to do some carpentry work on your house. This was not a licensed contractor. You gave this person $800 up front to buy materials, and after several days, no work has begun. Call the carpenter.   *R-te*

38. You need to find an attorney to help you with your immigration status. Call up the Lawyer Referral Service and ask the service to recommend someone.   *R-te*

39. You have had an interview for a job at an out-of-state company. You have not heard anything, and you are anxious to find out if you got the position. Call the company to find out your status.   *R-te*

40. Someone just had an accident on the freeway. Call the police from a call phone at the side of the road.   *R-te*

41. Call your employer and explain that you cannot come in to work today.   *R-te*

42. Your new puppy is lost. Call the Humane Society and find out if your dog is there.   *R-te*

43. Call and find out some information about a school you think you might want to attend.   *R-te*

44. Someone has been calling your number and making obscene sexual remarks. Call the phone company and see what can be done.   *R-te*

45. Someone calls you to sell you candy to benefit the blind. You are not interested in buying any at this time. What do you say?   *R-te*

46. An old lover is constantly calling you wanting you to get back together. Tell this person your relationship is over and to stop calling. *R-te*

47. Your elderly parent calls you daily to complain about you and your sibling. You have a family of your own, and would prefer if your parent called you less frequently. Talk to your parent about this the next time you receive a call. *R-te*

48. Telephone a florist and have some flowers delivered to a friend. *R-te*

49. You suspect your friend is not faithful to you. Call up a private investigator who you heard is supposed to be very good. *R-te*

50. You are working for a Crisis Hotline. You receive a call from someone who does not want to live anymore. What do you say? *R-te*

51. Your lover's parents are very conservative and don't know about you. When your lover leaves the house for a few minutes, the telephone rings and you pick it up. It is your lover's parents demanding to know where their child is and who you are. Talk to them. *R-te*

52. Call the phone number that was given to you when you bought your computer. Explain that you don't know much about computers and are having trouble setting it up. *R-te*

Thank you and Farewell

1. You are leaving the country. Thank your teacher for all the help and support you received while you were here. *R-thf*

2. Say good-bye to a good friend of yours who is returning to her native country. *R-thf*

3. There is a family crisis at home and you must return immediately. Say good-bye to your host family. *R-thf*

4. You are going back to your country. Say good-bye to someone you dated here in the US. *R-thf*

5. A close friend of yours has to return to his country because of family problems. Say good-bye to him. *R-thf*

6. Say good-bye to a close friend of yours whom you think you will never see again. *R-thf*

7. Say good-bye to a close friend of yours whom you feel you will probably meet again. *R-thf*

8. You have just been to a very enjoyable dinner party. Thank your host for inviting you and say good-bye. *R-thf*

9. Your friends are throwing you a going away party. They want you to make a speech. Thank them all for everything they have done and for being such good friends. *R-thf*

10. Say good-bye to someone you are breaking up with. *R-thf*

11. Say good-bye to your parents. You are going on a trip and may not return for a long time.   *R-thf*

12. Say good-bye to your classmate. Plan a meeting in one year's time.   *R-thf*

13. A friend has stayed with you for a few days. Say good-bye. *R-thf*

14. You have stayed with friends of your parents while you were on vacation. Thank the friends and invite them and their families to stay with you when they come to your country on vacation.   *R-thf*

15. Your friend is moving and comes to you to say good-bye. You are hoping that you will still remain friends. Say good-bye.   *R-thf*

16. A friend of yours gave you a bridal shower. As you are leaving, thank her.   *R-thf*

17. A man in your office has been fired. You don't think your boss was fair in firing him. Express sympathy, say good-bye, and wish the man good luck.   *R-thf*

17. You hear that a good friend of yours is dying. Visit your friend and say good-bye.   *R-thf*

18. Your six-year-old child is angry and wants to run away from home. He comes to say good-bye. Talk to him.   *R-thf*

19. You are going into the military. Thank your parents for everything they have done for you and say good-bye.   *R-thf*

20. For two years you have been the foster parent of a fifteen-year-old girl who is now returning to live with her mother. Say good-bye to the child.   *R-thf*

21. You called a neighbor last night to watch your child because you had to go to the hospital. You are home now and feeling much better. Go over and thank the neighbor.   *R-thf*

20. Someone came into your shop and bought a lot of merchandise. Thank the customer for coming in, encourage them to come back again, and say good-bye.   *R-thf*

Travel

1. Your sibling has just returned from a trip. Find out all about the trip.   *R-tr*

2. There is a family emergency and you need to buy an airline ticket immediately to get back to your hometown. At the airline ticket counter you are told that the airline has overbooked and you cannot get on a flight home. Talk to the person at the counter.   *R-tr*

3. You are thinking about taking a trip. Ask your friend where you ought to go.   *R-tr*

4. Try to convince your best friend to take a short vacation with you somewhere.   *R-tr*

5. You would like to take a trip to one of your classmates' countries. Ask your friend if you could stay at his family's house there. *R-tr*

6. Go to your travel agency. Ask an agent for information on tours. See if you can get an affordable tour package which would include hotel, meals, and transportation. *R-tr*

7. Your parent wants to take a trip with you, but you really would much rather spend the time with your friends. Talk to your parent. *R-tr*

8. Plan a trip with your best friend. Decide on how long to stay, where you will go, and how much money you will need. *R-tr*

9. Ask your hotel manager about the city you are visiting. Find out how and where you should go sightseeing. *R-tr*

10. While in another country, you lose all of your traveler's checks. Go to a bank and find out what you can do. *R-tr*

11. Having just arrived at your destination, you are waiting at customs and you can't seem to find your passport. Explain to the officials that you think it must have been stolen on the airplane. *R-tr*

12. You have forgotten to get a visa to come back into the US. Explain to the officials at the border that you are a student studying English in the US. *R-tr*

13. Tell the manager of a hotel that you think someone has been in your room. *R-tr*

14. You purchased a plane ticket at a travel agency. When you got home you realized it was made out for the wrong date. Tell the agent about this. *R-tr*

15. You think you have been over-charged for your hotel room. Speak to the hotel manager about this. *R-tr*

16. Ask your boss if you can take some time off and go on vacation. *R-tr*

17. Ask your spouse to take some time off from work and take a vacation with you. *R-tr*

18. Ask your friend where he usually goes on vacation, and why. *R-tr*

19. You have just gotten off a plane and you couldn't find your carry-on bag. You are sure you put it in the overhead compartment, and now it isn't there. Tell the attendant about your problem. *R-tr*

20. You have arrived at the airport just in time to be told that your seat has just been given to some-one else. What do you say? *R-tr*

21. You are traveling abroad and have arrived at your destination very late. You do not speak the language, all the banks are closed and you are unable to change your dollars into the new currency. Find a taxi and ex-plain to your driver (who doesn't speak much English) that you don't have any cur-rency of the country. *R-tr*

22. Your flight was cancelled and now you have to wait at the air-port four more hours for the next flight. Find someone who looks friendly so that you can talk with them and pass the time. *R-tr*

23. A woman and her son are sitting in a seat near you. For some rea-son the little boy won't let you alone. Talk to his mother. *R-tr*

24. You have been driving all night to reach your destination. When you arrive at the hotel where you made a reservation, you are told there is no reservation and there are no more rooms. Talk to the manager.   *R-tr*

25. Talk to your fiancé about where to go on your honeymoon.   *R-tr*

26. A co-worker of the opposite sex is accompanying you on a weekend business trip. Your spouse thinks you went alone. At the airport you meet one of your spouse's friends. Clearly she suspects you are having an affair. What do you say?   *R-tr*

27. You are going to Boston, but you have gotten on a plane to L.A. Ask the stewardess for help.   *R-tr*

28. You and your spouse would like to take a romantic vacation without the kids. Unfortunately, your children are looking forward to the family vacation. Talk to one of your children.   *R-tr*

29. You are on an eight-hour cruise with a friend whom you wanted to impress. After five hours of high waves, you are feeling seasick. Talk to your friend about what to do.   *R-tr*

30. You would like to join your friends who are taking a flight to the Caribbean. You are afraid of heights and have never been on a plane. Talk to your friend.   *R-tr*

31. You have arrived late from a flight that was supposed to connect with another flight. You have only five minutes to get to your next flight, and the gate is on the other side of the airport. Tell a flight attendant your problem and ask for help.   *R-tr*

32. The friend with whom you are traveling is driving you crazy. There is nothing your friend wants to do or see, and your friend does not leave you alone. Without making your friend feel bad, explain that you need to be by yourself.   *R-tr*

INTERVIEWS

The interview activity is based on a list of questions that can be used to draw out a wide variety of information, personal experience, and opinions.

Procedures for Interviews

#1. Two students come to the front of the room and speak for three minutes about the question on the card. One student initiates the interview with the question while the second responds. The interviewer can ask any additional questions to elicit more information. The other students listen and monitor the mistakes (see monitored conversation as described in the introduction).

#2. Group the students into pairs and have them discuss a card for three to five minutes. Give each pair a different card. Then ask the students to pass the card to the pair on their left. This procedure is repeated until each group has spoken about the question on each card. Circulate around the room, listening in on each pair and marking any mistakes on the mistake cards. After all the interview cards have been completed, the students look at their mistake cards and correct them. Circulate to assist with corrections.

#3. Divide the students into two or three groups, appointing one student as the leader of the group. The leader reads the interview card aloud to the group and must make sure that each student participates. Give each leader several cards and have them discuss each card for a specified amount of time. Collect the mistake cards of each group, and as you visit the group, write the mistakes of the speaker. When the interview cards are completed, hand back each student's mistake cards and ask the group to correct the mistakes together.

#4. Place the students into groups of four. Two students speak about the interview card question, while the other two monitor the mistakes in their notebooks. Then the two who were monitoring speak about the topic, while the other two students monitor them. After both pairs have spoken, the students go over the mistakes that they found.

#5. Have a group discussion of each interview card with no monitoring or correction. This can be done in pairs, small groups, or even a large classroom discussion. If some monitoring is desired, assign a few "monitors" whose job it is to record the mistakes of the students who speak.

#6. As an introduction to each topic (or even, if desired, each interview card), write a question on the blackboard and ask the students to write their answers in a specified amount of time (five to fifteen minutes). Collect the students' papers and then divide the students into groups to discuss what they wrote.

#7. As a follow-up, give a writing assignment after the cards have been discussed. If new vocabulary has been introduced, ask the students to use the new words or phrases. For variety, ask the students to write about another student's response.

The Arts

1. Do you feel that the arts are important? In what ways?   *I-ar*

2. Do you enjoy art? What kind of art do you prefer?   *I-ar*

3. In your opinion, who was/is the greatest artist in the world?   *I-ar*

4. Do you enjoy dancing or watching others dance? What kind of dancing do you enjoy the most?   *I-ar*

5. What is your opinion of the ballet?   *I-ar*

6. How do you feel about opera? Have you seen one? Why?   *I-ar*

7. Is it possible to dislike all music or have no sense of rhythm? *I-ar*

8. Do you prefer modern music over classical?   *I-ar*

9. What is your favorite instrument?   *I-ar*

10. Who are your favorite actors and actresses?   *I-ar*

11. Do you enjoy going to the theater? What kind?   *I-ar*

12. What kinds of movies do you prefer? Do you rent movies and play them at home, or do you enjoy going to the cinema? *I-ar*

13. Are you artistic? Why or why not?   *I-ar*

14. Have you ever participated in a talent show or play? Were you nervous?   *I-ar*

15. Do you have a favorite painter or photographer? Do you enjoy painting or taking photographs?   *I-ar*

16. Have you been to a museum in the last year? Why or why not?   *I-ar*

17. Do you enjoy going to the circus? Do you think the circus is an art form? What is your favorite circus act?   *I-ar*

18. Who was your favorite movie character when you were a child?   *I-ur*

19. Do you prefer going to a concert or staying at home and listening to music?   *I-ar*

20. Which musical groups are your favorite?   *I-ar*

21. Who is your favorite male or female vocalist?   *I-ar*

22. What do you think of country music? Rap music? Rock?   *I-ar*

23. Who was the greatest musical performer of all time?   *I-ar*

24. Would you enjoy the attention you would get being a performer, or would you prefer to have your privacy?   *I-ar*

25. Do you spend time reading about celebrities and their personal lives?   *I-ar*

26. Do you enjoy making things with your hands?   *I-ar*

27. Which form of literature do you prefer: Novels? Poetry? Drama? Short stories? Nonfiction?   *I-ar*

28. What are feelings about painting and sculpture?   *I-ar*

29. Do you like folk art? Why or why not? What do you mean when you say folk art?   *I-ar*

The Environment

1. What do you do to conserve natural resources? *I-en*

2. How can we stop the hunting of protected species of birds and animals? *I-en*

3. Which animals do you fear will become extinct in the next ten years? Twenty years? *I-en*

4. Why do you think there is so much air pollution from automobiles when the industry could be manufacturing cars that emit less pollution? Does this bother you? *I-en*

5. What can we individually do to help conserve energy and preserve the environment? What do you do? *I-en*

6. Which do you feel is more important, keeping workers employed in the lumber and wood industry or saving trees? Why? *I-en*

7. Do you think nuclear power plants are more dangerous than they are useful? *I-en*

8. How can we preserve our rainwater more efficiently? Are desalinization plants feasible? *I-en*

9. How can people encourage others to care about their environment and keep it clean? *I-en*

10. Do you think it is inevitable that humans will destroy the environment? Why or why not? *I-en*

11. Is it important to protect the rain forests? *I-en*

12. As land fills are used up, where will our wastes go? *I-en*

13. Are you concerned about the use of pesticides on fruits and vegetables? *I-en*

14. Do you wear furs and use leather? Do you feel using these products contributes to the cruelty of animals? *I-en*

15. Are you concerned with animal rights? *I-en*

16. Are there high enough penalties imposed on the people and companies illegally disposing of toxic wastes? *I-en*

17. Do you have a preference when it comes to choosing between organically grown fruits and vegetables and those that are chemically treated? Which do you prefer? *I-en*

18. Do you think artificial flavorings and colorings are bad for our health? *I-en*

19. Do you ever car pool? How can we get more people to use car pools? Do car pools exist in other countries? Do they help alleviate traffic congestion? *I-en*

20. Does the government work to protect the environment? In what ways? *I-en*

21. Do you think the number of natural disasters, such as earthquakes and floods, will increase or decrease in the next ten years? What can people do to become more prepared for these emergencies? *I-en*

22. Should companies be allowed to test new products on animals? *I-en*

23. Do you think animals should be used for human medical research? *I-en*

24. Do you think solar energy will ever be able to replace oil and gas? *I-en*

25. Do you think zoos and animal parks serve a worthwhile purpose? Why or why not? *I-en*

26. Do you worry about the ozone layer? Can anything be done to save it? *I-en*

27. Do we really need to have so much land devoted to national parks? Why or why not? *I-en*

28. Do you think most people care about what happens to the environment? *I-en*

29. When you see someone throw litter in the street, do you pick it up or leave it? Why? *I-en*

30. What do you think we can do to protect our environment for future generations? *I-en*

Family

1. What are some unusual things about your family? *I-fa*

2. What makes your family typical? Is this either good or bad? *I-fa*

3. Do you like children? What qualities about them do you like? *I-fa*

4. What irritates you about children? *I-fa*

5. Do you think it is better to be part of a large family or a small one? Why? *I-fa*

6. Is it better for a family to have a working mother or a mother who stays at home with the children? *I-fa*

7. What is the best way to punish a child? *I-fa*

8. Are there any forms of punishment that you would never implement? *I-fa*

9. What was your favorite book as a child? *I-fa*

10. What would be the ideal toy? *I-fa*

11. What was your favorite toy as a child? *I-fa*

12. Are there any toys that you would not permit your child to play with? *I-fa*

13. Do you think little girls and little boys should be treated differently? *I-fa*

14. Were you treated differently from a sibling of the opposite sex? *I-fa*

15. Do you think girls should play with "girl" toys and boys with "boy" toys? What happens if all the children play with all the toys? *I-fa*

16. Is anyone the head of your family? Should there be one? *I-fa*

17. Do you think grandparents have a positive or negative effect on the youngsters in a household? *I-fa*

18. Would you take in your aging father or mother to live with your family? *I-fa*

19. In what cases would you put your aging parent into a nursing home? *I-fa*

20. How many people constitute the ideal size for a family? *I-fa*

21. Is it better for children to live in a peaceful, single-parent household or in a two-parent household where the parents continually fight? Why? *I-fa*

22. Is there anything the people in your family could do to make your life easier? *I-fa*

23. Are you responsible if your child has psychological problems? *I-fa*

24. What causes the most problems in families today? *I-fa*

25. Do you think it is natural for men to be monogamous? *I-fa*

26. Is marriage a life-long commitment? *I-fa*

27. Would you encourage your child to marry someone of the same race? Would you discourage your child from marrying outside your race? *I-fa*

28. Would you ever consider adopting a child of another race? *I-fa*

29. Do you think you could be a foster parent? *I-fa*

30. Do you think joint custody works? *I-fa*

31. Is it appropriate for parents to walk around without clothes in front of their children? *I-fa*

32. Did your parents tell you anything about sex and masturbation? *I-fa*

33. Do you enjoy being with family at get-togethers or is it something you barely tolerate? *I-fa*

34. Do you feel that second cousins should be allowed to marry each other? *I-fa*

35. Do you think a parent is partly at fault if incest is going on in the family between a daughter and another family member? *I-fa*

36. Do you think it's right for a divorced stepfather to date his adopted stepdaughter? *I-fa*

37. Does your family have any "family secrets"? *I-fa*

38. What is the ideal age for having children? *I-fa*

39. What factors did you consider when thinking about having children? *I-fa*

40. Should parents be required to take a "parenting" class? *I-fa*

41. Why are there so many single-parent families nowadays? *I-fa*

42. What would you do if your child disappeared? *I-fa*

43. Do you think a homosexual couple should be allowed to adopt a child? *I-fa*

44. Were you encouraged to be independent as a child? Do you think it is an important quality? *I-fa*

Foreign Countries and Foreign Languages

1. Which foreign countries would you like to visit? Why? *I-ff*

2. In which country would you get the best education? *I-ff*

3. Are there any countries that you feel are dangerous to visit right now? Why? *I-ff*

4. In which countries do you feel the people are the most friendly? The most unfriendly? *I-ff*

5. In which country do you find the most job opportunities for someone in your field or with your interests? *I-ff*

6. Have you ever had pen pals? What country were they from? Would you like to have a pen-pal? From which country? *I-ff*

7. Would you like your child to speak many languages? Which ones? *I-ff*

8. Would you permit your child to study in another country? *I-ff*

9. Do you speak any foreign languages? Which foreign languages would you like to speak? Why? *I-ff*

10. Why is it so difficult for some people to learn a foreign language? *I-ff*

11. Are there any languages which sound melodious to you? Are there any languages which sound hard and abrasive? *I-ff*

12. Are there any countries you would prefer not to visit? Why? *I-ff*

13. Do you think it is good to have several different languages accepted and used within one country? Why or why not? *I-ff*

14. Do you think some languages are more difficult to learn than others? *I-ff*

15. Why is it so much easier for a child to learn a language than an adult? *I-ff*

16. Would you like to see more languages taught in school? *I-ff*

17. Should all children study foreign languages? At what age? *I-ff*

18. When you are traveling, do you try to speak the language of the country you are in? *I-ff*

19. Have you ever had a relationship with someone who did not speak your native language? *I-ff*

20. Is it more difficult to speak a language or to write it? To understand or to speak? To read or to write? Why? *I-ff*

Health

1. Why do you think studies show that women live longer than men? *I-he*

2. Why do you think married men tend to live longer than single men? *I-he*

3. Do you believe in homeopathic medicine? Have you ever been to a homeopath?   _I-he_

4. Do you take vitamins? Do you believe in taking mega-vitamins? What illnesses can vitamins fight?   _I-he_

5. Why do more women regularly go to the doctor than men? _I-he_

6. What do you do to prevent heart attacks?   _I-he_

7. Is it possible to control pain with breathing and meditation? _I-he_

8. Have you ever had a life-threatening disease or surgery?   _I-he_

9. Do you have health insurance? Should the US have health care coverage for all? How could we provide this?   _I-he_

10. Is there a link between what you eat and what diseases you will get? Can we prevent cancer through diet?   _I-he_

11. When a family member becomes terminally ill, whose decision should it be to take that person off life support?   _I-he_

12. Why are so many adolescents committing suicide?   _I-he_

13. Why are prescription drugs so costly in the US?   _I-he_

14. Do you receive better care if you belong to an HMO or have a private physician?   _I-he_

15. Do you think doctors are paid too much?   _I-he_

16. Do you have respect for your doctor? Why or why not?   _I-he_

17. Do you think everyone needs life insurance? Why or why not? _I-he_

18. Would you insist on being transported back to your country if you become very ill abroad?   _I-he_

19. Would you abort an unborn fetus if it had a genetic defect?   _I-he_

20. Are overweight people out of control, or is one's weight genetically determined at birth? _I-he_

21. Is homosexuality genetically determined, or is it socialized behavior or a matter of choice?_I-he_

22. Have you ever suffered from depression? Is depression an illness which causes the brain to malfunction, or does the brain malfunction and cause depression?   _I-he_

23. Why are so many people on antidepressants nowadays?   _I-he_

24. Have you ever known an addict? What do you think people can do to help loved ones who are addicted to illegal drugs? What would you do?   _I-he_

25. Which kinds of medical research do you feel need the most financial support? Is enough money being spent to find cures for cancer and heart disease?   _I-he_

26. Do you worry about AIDS for yourself or your children? Can we stop the spread of AIDS through education?   _I-he_

27. Why do you think so many women are getting breast cancer nowadays?   _I-he_

28. Within the next few years, what diseases will be cured?   _I-he_

29. Do you have mercury fillings? Do you think that mercury fillings in your teeth can cause health problems?   _I-he_

30. Do you smoke? What do you think of people who smoke? How would you help your child stop smoking?   *I-he*

31. Do you enjoy drinking alcohol? Do you think the restriction on selling alcohol to minors is effective?   *I-he*

32. What do you do to take care of yourself and stay physically healthy?   *I-he*

33. Do you think people who are dying from an incurable disease and are in great pain should be helped to die if they so choose?   *I-he*

34. What do you do to take care of your mental health? Do you believe psychologists and psychiatrists can help people overcome mental difficulties?   *I-he*

35. Did you practice prenatal care before the birth of your child? Is there any prenatal care a father can do?   *I-he*

36. Would you prefer to have a male doctor or a female doctor?   *I-he*

37. If someone has AIDS would you feel uncomfortable in the same room? Using the same public restroom?   *I-he*

38. When you are ill, do you trust your physician's judgment or do you seek out second opinions?   *I-he*

39. How do you explain illness and death to a small child? Did anyone ever explain it to you?   *I-he*

40. Are you afraid of going to the doctor or dentist? What is it you fear?   *I-he*

Interviewing for a Job

1. Tell me something about yourself.   *I-int*

2. What kind of position are you looking for?   *I-int*

3. What plans do you have for the future?   *I-int*

4. Tell me about your past job experiences.   *I-int*

5. Why did you leave your last job?   *I-int*

6. What did you think of your last boss?   *I-int*

7. Are you interested in temporary or permanent work?   *I-int*

8. Is salary important to you? *I-int*

9. Why do you want to work for our company?   *I-int*

10. Are you willing to relocate? *I-int*

11. Are you bondable?   *I-int*

12. Are you a self-starter?   *I-int*

13. How were you treated by your previous employers?   *I-int*

14. If we had recommendations from some of your previous employers, what would they say?   *I-int*

15. What are your strong points? *I-int*

16. What are your greatest weaknesses?   *I-int*

17. What do you think contributes to a person's advancement in a company?   *I-int*

18. Can you accept criticism from others?   *I-int*

19. What kinds of activities do you participate in?   *I-int*

20. What kinds of things do you like to read?   *I-int*

21. What was your favorite subject in school?   *I-int*

22. Do you have any special abilities which we should know about that would help you in this job?   *I-int*

23. How long are you planning to stay with our company?   *I-int*

24. What did you dislike most in school?   *I-int*

25. What did you like least about your previous job/employer?   *I-int*

26. Why should I hire you?   *I-int*

27. What can you do for our company?   *I-int*

28. Do you know anything about our company?   *I-int*

29. Why have you been out of work for so long?   *I-int*

30. Do you have any questions you would like to ask us?   *I-int*

Laughter

1. What kinds of things do you laugh at?   *I-la*

2. Do you ever laugh at people who are physically or mentally handicapped? Why?   *I-la*

3. What kinds of jokes do you like?   *I-la*

4. Do you like slapstick comedy?   *I-la*

5. Who are your favorite comedians or comic strips?   *I-la*

6. Do you think you're funny? Why or why not?   *I-la*

7. Do others think you're funny? Why is that?   *I-la*

8. Do people in your country laugh at things that are different from the people in this country?   *I-la*

9. How do you laugh? Are you inhibited or do you let go?   *I-la*

10. Is having a good sense of humor important? Why or why not?   *I-la*

11. Why do you think some people laugh at others?   *I-la*

12. In what situations do you use laughter as an outlet? Does it help?   *I-la*

13. What kinds of people look funny to you?   *I-la*

14. What is the funniest movie you've ever seen?   *I-la*

15. Do you like watching American situation comedies?   *I-la*

16. Do you think women are funnier than men?   *I-la*

17. What are some funny things children do?   *I-la*

18. What are some funny things pets do?   *I-la*

19. Do you ever laugh out loud when you are alone? *I-la*

20. Have you ever laughed so hard that you cried? When? What were you laughing at? *I-la*

21. Do you enjoy reading "the funnies" in the newspaper? *I-la*

22. Are stand-up comics funnier when you watch them live on stage or on TV? *I-la*

Law and Justice

1. Do you believe the law should decide whether a woman can abort her unborn child? Do you believe in the right to choose? *I-lj*

2. Do you think our present prison system is a good deterrent for potential criminals? If you could, what would you do to change it? *I-lj*

3. Do you believe in capital punishment? *I-lj*

4. What should be done with convicted rapists? Repeat rapists? Serial killers? Drunk drivers? Repeat drunk drivers? *I-lj*

5. Would you want to know if a convicted child molester moves into your neighborhood after serving time in prison, or does the molester have a right to privacy? *I-lj*

6. Is there anything wrong with looking at pornography? Should certain types of pornography be censored? *I-lj*

7. Do you believe minorities in the United States are treated equally under the law? *I-lj*

8. Do famous people have the right to privacy, or do photographers have the right to follow these people and take their pictures? *I-lj*

9. Do you think crime would be reduced if narcotics were made legal and the government gave them to addicts free? *I-lj*

10. Do governments have the right to ban smoking in public places? Would you approve of this ban? *I-lj*

11. Do you think security guards at your children's schools should be allowed to carry weapons? *I-lj*

12. What do you think of the use of the insanity defense? Is a person innocent if they were insane when they committed a crime? *I-lj*

13. Have you ever sued someone or been sued? Is it too easy to sue nowadays? *I-lj*

14. Should trials of celebrities be broadcast on TV? Is this entertaining to you? *I-lj*

15. Do you want the government to use your tax money to pay for the education and hospitalization of illegal immigrants? *I-lj*

16. How did your family come to America? Would you prefer the law to crack down on immigration, or to allow more immigrants in? *I-lj*

17. Do you think our present laws regarding adoption and foster care are working? *I-lj*

18. Do you think juveniles should be tried as adults? At what age? Would you take into account the crime?   *I-lj*

19. What if your child wanted to divorce you? Should children be allowed to sue parents for divorce?   *I-lj*

20. Do you like lawyers? Why do so many people in the US distrust lawyers? Is it that way in other countries?   *I-lj*

21. What privacy rights do you think prisoners should have in jail? *I-lj*

22. Should prisoners be allowed to study law while they're imprisoned? Work out? Read? Watch TV? Play tennis? Have conjugal privileges?   *I-lj*

23. What do you think of the parole system? Do you know anyone who is out on parole?   *I-lj*

24. How do you feel about prisoners using tax dollars to sue prisons in order to get more comfortable quarters and better food?   *I-lj*

25. Do you think our criminal system protects our society or worries too much about the rights of the accused?   *I-lj*

26. What do you think of our present prison system?   *I-lj*

27. Have you ever been arrested? Do you know anyone who has? Do you think the American legal system is better or worse, compared with what you have heard about other countries?   *I-lj*

28. Do you feel the tax system is fair? Do you think there are too many loopholes for the wealthy?   *I-lj*

29. Are there some people that cannot be rehabilitated?   *I-lj*

30. Can convicted criminals ever really change? Should they be given the opportunity to help society? In what way?   *I-lj*

31. What kind of retribution should convicts have to pay to their victims?   *I-lj*

32. Do you have any ideas on how to improve the legal system?

33. Do you think some people are born criminals?   *I-lj*

34. Do you feel safe in the streets? Are there enough police officers? Are you afraid of the police or do you feel safer around them?   *I-lj*

35. How would you like the law to deal with vandals who deface property with graffiti?   *I-lj*

36. Do you think vigilantes are criminals or heros?   *I-lj*

37. Have you ever called the police? What would you like to see the police do differently to help stop crime?   *I-lj*

38. Have you ever witnessed household violence? How can we protect the victims from household violence when the victims refuse to cooperate with the law?   *I-lj*

39. Have you ever been or known a gang member? What would you suggest can be done to stop drive-by shootings and to eradicate gang violence?   *I-lj*

40. Do you own a weapon? Do you feel more comfortable taking your weapon with you or being without it?   *I-lj*

41. If someone broke into your house do you think you would be able to protect yourself? *I-lj*

Men, Women, and Relationships

1. Have you tried any American dating customs? Which ones? How do you feel about them? *I-mwr*

2. Who should pay for a date, the man or the woman? *I-mwr*

3. At what age do you think your child should be allowed to go out on a date? *I-mwr*

4. At what age did you go out on your first date? *I-mwr*

5. What are the best ways of finding a date? What did you do? *I-mwr*

6. Have you ever used any "come ons" to get a date? *I-mwr*

7. Do you think parents should be involved in choosing a mate for their children? Would you like to be involved in choosing someone for your child? *I-mwr*

8. Do you know when someone is flirting with you? How? *I-mwr*

9. Do you enjoy flirting? What do you like about it? *I-mwr*

10. What is the bst way for youths to find out about sex? *I-mwr*

11. How did you learn about sex?

12. Are men and women's brains different? In what ways? *I-mwr*

13. Do you think men and women should be treated equally in all aspects of life? *I-mwr*

14. Are men and women capable of performing the same jobs? *I-mwr*

15. Do you get along better with men or women? *I-mwr*

16. Do you think women can fight as well as men in military combat? *I-mwr*

17. Is there anything you dislike about the opposite sex? *I-mwr*

18. Which do you think it's easier to be, a man or a woman? a father or a mother? *I-mwr*

19. Do you think a man should feel it's acceptable to show his feelings and, if necessary, cry in public? *I-mwr*

20. Do you really consider a couple who has no children a family?

21. Does having children put a strain on a relationship or make it easier? How? *I-mwr*

22. Do you think the bodies of female body builders are attractive? What about male bodybuilders? *I-mwr*

23. Do you think women have a more difficult time with their weight than men? Why? *I-mwr*

24. Do you think a person's sexual orientation is determined at birth? Can it be changed? *I-mwr*

25. Would you want a woman president of the US? Why or why not? *I-mwr*

26. Do men and women express love differently? *I-mwr*

27. Do you think men enjoy sex more than women? *I-mwr*

28. Do women want commitment more than men? Why? *I-mwr*

29. Is it easier for men to lie than women? Is lying just a part of any relationship? *I-mwr*

30. Do you think it's more tolerable for men to have affairs than it is for women? *I-mwr*

31. What do you think of women with much older men? Of women with much younger men? Of men with much older women? Of men with much younger women? *I-mwr*

32. Which would you prefer to be, the person who breaks up a relationship or the person whose relationship is broken up. Why? *I-mwr*

33. Do females enjoy pornography as much as men? Have you ever rented adult movies or gone to a porno movie? *I-mwr*

34. Do you think about sex a lot? Do you fantasize? Do you think sexual fantasies are good or bad for a relationship? *I-mwr*

35. What is your definition of "love"? Have you ever been in love? *I-mwr*

36. Are you ever certain that you are marrying the right person? *I-mwr*

37. Can a man be friends with a woman, or is there always something sexual involved? *I-mwr*

38. Do women make better friendships than men? Are most of your friends male or female? *I-mwr*

39. Can a person remain friends with an ex-lover after the relationship has ended? Have you ever been able to do this? *I-mwr*

40. How would you compare your past relationships? *I-mwr*

41. Is it natural for people to be monogamous? *I-mwr*

42. Do people need to be married? What is the best age for a person to get married? How old were you? *I-mwr*

43. What is the ideal age to begin raising children? *I-mwr*

44. Do you think it is better to live with your partner before marriage? Did you? *I-mwr*

45. Why do you think so many couples are getting divorced nowadays? *I-mwr*

46. In your experience, who complains more, men or women? *I-mwr*

47. How have the roles of men and women changed since you were a child? How will the roles change by the time your children are grown? *I-mwr*

48. Are men naturally more aggressive than women? *I-mwr*

49. Do you know any gay couples? Can two people of the same sex have a loving, sexual relationship? *I-mwr*

Minorities

1. Are there any business opportunities for minorities in your native country? *I-mi*

2. Have you ever felt racial prejudice or discrimination directed against you? *I-mi*

3. What are the stereotypes of minorities you have? How do you think stereotypes develop? *I-mi*

4. What do you think causes racial prejudice? *I-mi*

5. Were there any stereotypes you were brought up with as a child that have made you feel a certain way about a racial group? *I-mi*

6. What are the different minorities in your country? How are they perceived by the majority of the population? *I-mi*

7. Is there racial prejudice in your country? Why do you think it exists? *I-mi*

8. Are there any organizations in your country that exist to fight or promote racial discrimination and segregation? *I-mi*

9. What kinds of discrimination exist in your country? Why? *I-mi*

10. Is there a "privileged" class in your country? Why? *I-mi*

11. Do any minorities in your country hold an elected office? Do any hold appointed office? *I-mi*

12. Do you think the US could do anything to make black and white relations better? What? *I-mi*

13. Do you think we should have segregated schools? Do you agree or disagree with busing? *I-mi*

14. Do you think the US will ever have a president who is not Caucasian? *I-mi*

15. Are African Americans and white Americans perceived in the same way in your native country? How are they perceived differently? *I-mi*

16. Do you think it is easier to be white or black in the US? *I-mi*

17. Do you think there are any inborn differences between blacks and whites? *I-mi*

18. Why do you think the US has so many racial problems? *I-mi*

19. What do you think of affirmative action? Have you ever gotten a job only because the company needed a "token" minority? *I-mi*

20. Do you think the government should allow organizations to threaten to destroy other races and minorities? *I-mi*

21. Are you frightened by any minority groups? Why? *I-mi*

22. Do you think minorities are exploited in the United States? In what ways? *I-mi*

23. Have you ever been involved with racial violence? What kinds of things instigate this type of violence? *I-mi*

24. What do you think of the "skinhead" movement? *I-mi*

25. Where in the US would you think race riots with burning, looting, and killing could occur? *I-mi*

26. Why does "gay bashing" persist? Does this exist in all countries? *I-mi*

27. Should homosexuals be excluded from the teaching profession, nursing, and other fields of work? Would you want a homosexual to be your child's teacher? *I-mi*

28. Have you ever met an American Indian? Do you think they are treated better or worse than other minorities? *I-mi*

29. What are the real differences between racial minorities, religious minorities, or sexual minorities?   *I-mi*

30. Do you think it is better for a country to have a society with minorities or a society that is more homogeneous? Why? *I-mi*

Native Country

1. How does this city compare to your native city?   *I-na*

2. Why did you leave your country to come here?   *I-na*

3. What are some interesting things about your native country?   *I-na*

4. What do you miss most about your native country?   *I-na*

5. What do you dislike about your country?   *I-na*

6. Do you prefer living here or in your country?   *I-na*

7. Where do you think it is better to raise children, in your country or the US?   *I-na*

8. Do you think people are friendlier in your country?   *I-na*

9. Whom do you miss the most from your country?   *I-na*

10. What do you think of the political system in your country? *I-na*

11. What was your daily routine like in your native country?   *I-na*

12. Are there any injustices in your country that you would like to see corrected? What are they?   *I-na*

13. What were some of the hardships in your native country?   *I-na*

14. What are some of the major differences in customs between the US and your native land?   *I-na*

15. Is there a great disparity between the rich and the poor in your country? Why?   *I-na*

16. Were you encouraged to travel to the US? By whom and why? *I-na*

17. Did you experience "culture shock" when you first arrived from your native land?   *I-na*

18. Are you planning to return to your home country or would you prefer to remain here?   *I-na*

19. What opportunities for living and working are there in your country for a foreigner?   *I-na*

20. Do you have many tourists visiting your country? How are they treated? Where do they go? *I-na*

People

1. Why do so many people not want to get involved with others and their problems? What is your position on getting involved?   *I-pe*

2. Has life been disappointing for you? Why do some people continually complain that they are disappointed in life and by others?   *I-pe*

3. What physical characteristics make a person beautiful? What mental characteristics?   *I-pe*

4. Did you have a hero as a child? Do you have one now?   *I-pe*

5. Why do some people hate others? Is there anyone you truly hate?   *I-pe*

6. Why do some people have no friends? How important is friendship?   *I-pe*

7. Would the world be a better place to live if some people weren't in it? Who?   *I-pe*

8. Do you put a lot of emphasis in your life on money and power?   *I-pe*

9. Can you forgive and forget? Why do people have such a hard time forgiving others?   *I-pe*

10. Are you religious? Why do different groups argue about religion?   *I-pe*

11. Is any cause worth dying for? *I-pe*

12. Are you a lucky person? Do you know anyone who is? Why?   *I-pe*

13. Who do you think is the most powerful person in the world? Why?   *I-pe*

14. In your lifetime, who has influenced the course of history the most?   *I-pe*

15. Do you tend to give up easily or do you continue to try?   *I-pe*

16. Are there certain personality types in which we can categorize all people? What type would you say you are?   *I-pe*

17. Why do some people enjoy being with others and some prefer to be alone?   *I-pe*

18. Why are some people popular, while others are always unpopular?   *I-pe*

19. Have you ever known anyone who was charismatic? What qualities make a person charismatic?   *I-pe*

20. What attributes are the most important to you in a person? *I-pe*

21. Are some people born evil? *I-pe*

22. Can people ever truly change? Have you ever known someone to change?   *I-pe*

23. Why do so many people feel alienated by society?   *I-pe*

24. How many children should a family have? Does anyone have the right to limit the size of the family?   *I-pe*

25. Does anyone have the right to determine when another person will die?   *I-pe*

26. In what ways are all people the same? In what ways different?   *I-pe*

27. How important is the influence of genes on the development of a person's personality?   *I-pe*

28. Why do people fear the things they don't understand?   *I-pe*

29. Why is it so important to feel accepted by others?   *I-pe*

30. For some people, why are possessions more important than people?   *I-pe*

Personal Data

1. Are you a day person or a night person?   *I-pd*

2. Do you live in the past, present or future?   *I-pd*

3. Do you prefer to work with people, data or machines? *I-pd*

4. What is your favorite animal? *I-pd*

5. What would your friends say are your best qualities?   *I-pd*

6. How do you relax?   *I-pd*

7. What are your pet peeves? *I-pd*

8. Are you a procrastinator?   *I-pd*

9. Are you usually energetic or lazy?   *I-pd*

10. Do you have any favorite hobbies? What are they?   *I-pd*

11. What is your favorite food? *I-pd*

12. What is your least favorite food?   *I-pd*

13. Do you prefer to be a spectator or a participant?   *I-pd*

14. What is something you know how to do really well?   *I-pd*

15. Are you an optimist or a pessimist?   *I-pd*

16. What is your favorite color?*I-pd*

17. What one scientific invention could you not live without? *I-pd*

18. What is your most prized possession?   *I-pd*

19. Why are you studying English?   *I-pd*

20. What part of nature do you like most?   *I-pd*

21. Do you prefer living near the ocean or the mountains?   *I-pd*

22. Do you love yourself? Why or why not?   *I-pd*

23. How do you make yourself fall asleep? In what position are you the most comfortable?   *I-pd*

24. Do you belong to any clubs or organizations?   *I-pd*

25. Do you ever talk to yourself? What do you say?   *I-pd*

26. Are you a jealous person?   *I-pd*

27. What are some things which make you angry?   *I-pd*

28. What makes you cry?   *I-pd*

29. What is your favorite day of the week?   *I-pd*

30. What is the most productive time of the day for you?   *I-pd*

31. Do you have a favorite holiday? Which one and why?   *I-pd*

32. Do you like to travel or to stay at home?   *I-pd*

33. What is your favorite kind of entertainment?   *I-pd*

34. What are some of the similarities among people you like?   *I-pd*

35. Who was the greatest person who ever lived? Why do you think so?   *I-pd*

36. Is there a famous person you'd have a lot in common with? *I-pd*

37. Do you think with your mind or your heart?   *I-pd*

38. Do you consider yourself to be an average person or an extraordinary person?   *I-pd*

39. Do you believe in psychics or fortune tellers? Why?   *I-pd*

40. Do you believe in fate?   *I-pd*

Personal Values

1. What is the one thing you would like to change about yourself?   *I-pv*

2. What are some human values that you really believe in?   *I-pv*

3. What's necessary in life?   *I-pv*

4. How important are material things in your life?   *I-pv*

5. Do you like to play? Do you play to win?   *I-pv*

6. Are you really satisfied with your life?   *I-pv*

7. How important for you is it to be right?   *I-pv*

8. Are you a spiritual person? Do you believe in God?   *I-pv*

9. What are the things you want most in life?   *I-pv*

10. What is one important thing you would like to accomplish in your life?   *I-pv*

11. What is the hardest obstacle in your life?   *I-pv*

12. What causes you the greatest despair?   *I-pv*

13. What is the one thing that you hope to continue throughout your life?   *I-pv*

14. Do you have a personal motto that you try to live by?   *I-pv*

15. What is the most important contribution you have given to society?   *I-pv*

16. What has been your greatest achievement?   *I-pv*

17. What has been your greatest failure?   *I-pv*

18. Which is harder for you to endure, physical pain or mental pain?   *I-pv*

19. Would you want to know the exact date and time of your own death?   *I-pv*

20. How would you prefer to die?   *I-pv*

21. How would you like to be remembered?   *I-pv*

Personal Experience

1. Have you ever made a decision that you knew was wrong the minute you made it but was too late to change?   *I-pex*

2. What have you done in your free time that you enjoyed the least? Why did you do this?   *I-pex*

3. Where did you spend your best vacation?   *I-pex*

4. Is there any special place that you used to go as a child to escape those around you?   *I-pex*

5. How far back into your childhood can you remember?   *I-pex*

6. Did you have any childhood loves?   *I-pex*

7. Have you ever thought up a wonderful invention?   *I-pex*

8. Have you ever told a lie that you couldn't get out of?   *I-pex*

9. Have you ever had to go to the police station?   *I-pex*

10. Do you ever feel that God is with you?   *I-pex*

11. Is there anything that you tried at one time that you will never try again?   *I-pex*

12. Is there some smell, taste, or sound that reminds you of something you knew as a child?   *I-pex*

13. Do you have any recurring dreams?   *I-pex*

14. Have you ever experienced *déjà vu?*   *I-pex*

15. Can you remember a nightmare you had?   *I-pex*

16. Have you ever been cheated by someone?   *I-pex*

17. Have you ever had to escape from somewhere?   *I-pex*

18. Have you ever not been able to find something that was very important?   *I-pex*

19. Have you ever been able to stop an accident before it occurred, but didn't?   *I-pex*

20. Did you ever do anything to save someone's life?   *I-pex*

21. Have you ever had a near death experience?   *I-pex*

22. Have you ever had someone rob you?   *I-pex*

23. Did you ever have a premonition that turned out to be true? *I-pex*

24. Have you ever seen or heard ghosts or voices from the past?   *I-pex*

25. Have you ever taken a really bad vacation?   *I-pex*

26. Have you ever been really hurt by someone, physically or emotionally?   *I-pex*

27. Were you ever fired from a job?   *I-pex*

Politics

1. What do you think of the American form of government?   *I-po*

2. Are you a conservative or a liberal?   *I-po*

3. Do you think there is too much government these days?   *I-po*

4. Do you vote? Why do so many people refuse to do so?   *I-po*

5. Are there any injustices in this country that you would like to see corrected?   *I-po*

6. Are political parties necessary? How many should there be? *I-po*

7. Is there much difference between a Republican and a Democrat? What are the differences?   *I-po*

8. What are some of the injustices that you are aware of in the US?   *I-po*

9. Do you think politics should be discussed in schools?   *I-po*

10. What is your idea of a perfect society?   *I-po*

11. Do you think we will have a third world war?   *I-po*

12. Do you think human beings are violent by nature? *I-po*

13. What do you think can be done to prevent a nuclear war? *I-po*

14. Do you think that the United States is still the most powerful country in the world? *I-po*

15. Should private industry be allowed to contribute large sums of money to political candidates? *I-po*

16. Are all politicians corrupt? *I-po*

17. Should terms of public office be limited? What would be the limits? *I-po*

18. Do you have to be rich to be a political leader in the US? *I-po*

19. Why are governments so bureaucratic? *I-po*

20. Which country do you think has the most efficient political system? Why? *I-po*

School

1. How would you teach this class differently? *I-sch*

2. Do you like to study? *I-sch*

3. Did you like school as a child? What was your favorite subject in school? *I-sch*

4. What was your least favorite subject? Who was your least favorite teacher? *I-sch*

5. What are the most important qualities in a good teacher? *I-sch*

6. What characteristics do you dislike in a teacher? *I-sch*

7. What is the most effective way for you to study? *I-sch*

8. Is there something you learned in school that you find totally useless now? *I-sch*

9. How important do you think a college education is nowadays? *I-sch*

10. Do you think that children get more of an education inside the classroom working with a teacher or outside with their friends? *I-sch*

11. How much should parents teach their children in the home? What should they teach? *I-sch*

12. Did you have a favorite teacher as a child? Who was it? *I-sch*

13. Should children be taught religion in school? *I-sch*

14. Should a teacher be permitted to teach in any other language besides English? *I-sch*

15. Which country has the best educational system? Why? *I-sch*

16. What are some of the problems with public education in the US? *I-sch*

17. Would your child be safe in a public school anywhere in the US? Why or why not? *I-sch*

18. At what age do you think a child is old enough to make the decision to drop out of school? *I-sch*

19. Why are so many high school graduates functionally illiterate? *I-sch*

20. Why are teachers paid such low salaries? *I-sch*

21. Do you think people value education enough in our society? *I-sch*

22. What kinds of problems could be eased in our society by education? *I-sch*

23. What kind of education did your parents have? *I-sch*

24. How do you relate to people with a lower educational background? *I-sch*

25. What types of things are not taught in school but should be taught? *I-sch*

26. Is it appropriate for teachers to teach students about human sexual behavior? *I-sch*

27. Would you object if a homosexual was your child's teacher? What if the teacher was someone with AIDS? *I-sch*

28. Do you think home study is more effective than public or private schooling? Why or why not? *I-sch*

29. Should teachers be allowed to give students homework? How much is too much? *I-sch*

30. Would you feel uncomfortable if your children complained that their teacher touched them too much? *I-sch*

31. Would you prefer your child be taught by a male instructor or a female? Why? *I-sch*

32. Should parents help children with their homework? *I-sch*

33. What rights do students have in school? *I-sch*

34. What can be done to keep violence out of schools? *I-sch*

35. If your child were intellectually gifted, would you prefer to have your child placed only with students of the same high intelligence? *I-sch*

36. Do you think students with learning disabilities should be in special classes with other learning disabled students, or placed in ordinary classes? *I-sch*

37. How should parents be involved in school? Why? *I-sch*

38. What can be done about continual disruption and disobedience in the classroom? *I-sch*

Sports

1. What sports do you enjoy the most? What is it about them that you enjoy? *I-sp*

2. Were you encouraged as a child to play sports? *I-sp*

3. Were you ever injured while engaging in sports? *I-sp*

4. Which sports are too dangerous for children? *I-sp*

5. Are there any sports that should be made illegal? *I-sp*

6. How important are sports to a child's development? *I-sp*

7. Do you enjoy going to sports events? Which ones? *I-sp*

8. Do you feel some sports are really for men and others for women? *I-sp*

9. Do you prefer to play team sports or individual sports? *I-sp*

10. Who are your favorite athletes? Are they all pros? *I-sp*

11. Do you watch sports on TV? Which ones? *I-sp*

12. Do you watch the Olympics? Which sports do you find the most interesting to watch? *I-sp*

13. Are there any sports you have tried but just can't do? *I-sp*

14. What kind of person becomes an Olympian? *I-sp*

15. Have you ever participated in a marathon? Would you like to? What is stopping you? *I-sp*

16. Do you think anyone could become a professional athlete with the proper training? *I-sp*

17. Do you think there is too much emphasis on college sports? *I-sp*

18. Do you think professional athletes are paid too much money? Why? *I-sp*

19. In the next few years, do you think soccer could replace baseball as the number one sport in the United States? *I-sp*

20. What do you think is the most popular sport in the world today? In your native country? In the US? *I-sp*

21. Does one race produce better athletes than other races? *I-sp*

22. Do you think athletes should be allowed to enhance their performance with drugs? What drugs should they be tested for? How often? *I-sp*

23. What is the most beautiful sport to watch? *I-sp*

24. What is the most exciting sport to play? *I-sp*

Television

1. What are the positive and the negative effects of television on children? *I-tv*

2. Do you think that our present rating system for movies is good? Why or why not? *I-tv*

3. What do you think of American TV commercials? In your country are the ads different? *I-tv*

4. Do you think commercials ought to be permitted on children's TV shows? What kinds of commercials would be appropriate? *I-tv*

5. Do TV programs present a realistic picture of American life? Why or why not? *I-tv*

6. Do you think television is an effective baby sitter? *I-tv*

7. Should children have unrestricted use of the TV set? *I-tv*

8. How many TV sets are there in your home? How many would you like to have? Why? *I-tv*

9. Are TV shows better or worse in other countries? *I-tv*

10. How important is watching television in another language when you are studying that language? *I-tv*

11. Think of your earliest TV memories. How has TV changed? *I-tv*

12. Do you think some people are influenced to commit crimes because of TV? *I-tv*

13. What kinds of shows do you and your family usually watch? *I-tv*

14. Do you usually watch TV with other people or by yourself? *I-tv*

15. Do you eat more when you watch TV? What do you eat? *I-tv*

16. What kinds of TV shows do you dislike? Why? *I-tv*

17. Do you usually sit through commercials? If not, what do you do at these times? *I-tv*

18. Do you believe that commercials show you the truth? *I-tv*

19. How can we change American TV so that we can make it a better use of our time? *I-tv*

20. Do you think public broadcasting is better than privately owned broadcasting? Why? *I-tv*

21. Can you do other things when you are watching TV? What do you usually do? *I-tv*

22. Do you think the news programs on TV are accurate? Are some better than others? Why? *I-tv*

What If?

1. If you could be anyone in the world, who would you be? *I-wh*

2. If you could be doing anything you choose right now, what would you want to do? *I-wh*

3. If you had been a much different height, how would your life have been different? *I-wh*

4. If you had been a different weight as a child, how would your life have been different? *I-wh*

5. If you were rich, how would your life be different? *I-wh*

6. If you could be any age, what age would you be? Why? *I-wh*

7. If you could live anywhere in the world, where would you choose to live? *I-wh*

8. If you could have anything in the world you wanted, what would you ask for? *I-wh*

9. If you could change one thing about yourself, what would you change? *I-wh*

10. If you hadn't come to the US, how would life be different? *I-wh*

11. If you could do one thing to change the world, what would you do? *I-wh*

12. If you could change one thing about someone else, who and what would you change? *I-wh*

13. If you were president, how would you change the US? *I-wh*

14. If you had been born a different sex, how would your life have been different? *I-wh*

15. If you'd been born poor, how would your life have been different? *I-wh*

16. If you could bring one person back to life, who would that be? *I-wh*

17. If you could live forever, would you choose to do so? *I-wh*

18. If you could be a famous person, who would you want to be? *I-wh*

19. If you could genetically engineer your children, would you? *I-wh*

20. If you could learn one more skill, what would that be? *I-wh*

21. If you could create a perfect world, what kind of world would it be? *I-wh*

22. If you could create the perfect mate for yourself, what kind of person would that be? *I-wh*

23. If you could live in any time period (past, present, future), when would you want to live? *I-wh*

24. If you had three wishes, what would you ask for? *I-wh*

25. If you had to decide between wealth or happiness, which would you choose? *I-wh*

Work

1. Would you prefer to have a male supervisor or a female supervisor? Why? *I-wk*

2. What kinds of questions do you think an employer should not ask an employee? What does an employer need to know about an employee and why? *I-wk*

3. What kinds of jobs are you suited for? Why? *I-wk*

4. What kinds of job would you hate? Why? *I-wk*

5. Are you more comfortable working with other people or by yourself? *I-wk*

6. Would you sacrifice your job for the sake of your integrity? *I-wk*

7. When you work, are you more productive listening to music or working in silence? *I-wk*

8. When you are on the job, who are you trying to please more, yourself or your employer? *I-wk*

9. Would you feel uncomfortable working next to someone of the opposite sex in certain jobs? Which ones? *I-wk*

10. Which is more important to you, making lots of money or enjoying your job? *I-wk*

11. Do you prefer to work fewer days and longer hours, or more days and fewer hours? *I-wk*

12. Do you think unemployment benefits are too high and last too long? *I-wk*

13. Would you prefer to work for yourself in a risky business or to work for someone else in a more stable business? *I-wk*

14. What kinds of skills for the job market do you wish you had learned when you were younger? Is it too late for you to learn these skills now? *I-wk*

15. Do you continue working at something even when you are frustrated, or do you give up easily? *I-wk*

16. All work has some unpleasant aspects? How do you deal with them in your work? *I-wk*

17. Do you like getting feedback and evaluations from your boss? Does it help you? *I-wk*

18. Are you uncomfortable asking for a raise even when you know you deserve it? Why? *I-wk*

19. Are there unions to join in your field? Do you join them? *I-wk*

TALKS

The topics in this activity stimulate self-expression. Some of the topics require the students to talk about themselves, share personal experiences, and express hopes and opinions. The *Truth or Lies* topic requires the students to make some decisions based on their own individual code of ethics and values. The *Comparisons* and *Time Travel* topics are less personal. They challenge the imagination and can be used to stimulate factual and intellectual expression.

Procedures for Talks

#1. Have each student choose a card. Then pair up the students and give each pair about 15-20 minutes to talk about their cards in free conversation. Questions are encouraged, as well as expansion of the topic through other related experiences.

After this is completed, instruct one student in each pair to speak for three to five minutes on his card, while the other student times and monitors the errors. When this is completed, the other student speaks and the procedure is reversed.

Finally, call up each student to speak on his card in front of the class for three to five minutes. During the talks, write the mistakes on the student's mistake cards. After each student speaks, encourage the other students to ask questions as well as relate their own experiences. Correction of errors can be done following the class discussion.

#2. *Variations:* Have the students prepare their talks for homework. They should make some notes to help them with their presentations. They can practice in class with a partner who will monitor the mistakes before the presentations are given to the entire class.

#3. These topics can be used as a writing assignment before or after they have been used in class.

Comparisons

1. Compare this country with your native country. *T-cm*

2. Compare two powerful people. *T-cm*

3. Compare being single and being married. *T-cm*

4. Compare two different fruits. *T-cm*

5. Compare Heaven and Hell. *T-cm*

6. Compare men and women. *T-cm*

7. Compare what it's like to be famous with what it's like to be infamous. *T-cm*

8. Compare two presidents of the United States. *T-cm*

9. Compare the politics of the United States with the politics of another country. *T-cm*

10. Compare life nowadays with life twenty years ago. *T-cm*

11. Compare your mother with your father. *T-cm*

12. Compare your two sets of grandparents. *T-cm*

13. Compare rock music and classical music. *T-cm*

14. Compare your children. *T-cm*

15. Compare flowers with weeds. *T-cm*

16. Compare living alone with living with someone. *T-cm*

17. Compare doctors and lawyers. *T-cm*

18. Compare fingers and toes. *T-cm*

19. Compare being ashamed and being embarrassed. *T-cm*

20. Compare comedy and tragedy. *T-cm*

21. Compare life and death. *T-cm*

22. Compare the moon and the sun. *T-cm*

23. Compare a white collar worker with a blue collar worker. *T-cm*

24. Compare children with parents. *T-cm*

25. Compare casual clothes with formal attire. *T-cm*

26. Compare a cat and a dog. *T-cm*

27. Compare your ability in writing and speaking English. *T-cm*

28. Compare sorrow and despair. *T-cm*

29. Compare two sports. *T-cm*

30. Compare a child's experience of being with a baby sitter and being in day care. *T-cm*

31. Compare two of your friends. *T-cm*

32. Compare two people you do not like. *T-cm*

33. Compare two of your teachers. *T-cm*

34. Compare loneliness and being alone. *T-cm*

35. Compare two holidays. *T-cm*

36. Compare the culture of two countries. *T-cm*

37. Compare the topography of the state in which you live to the topography of another state. *T-cm*

38. Compare two different religions. *T-cm*

39. Compare education in a developing country to that of a developed country.   *T-cm*

40. Compare the prices in the United States to the prices in your native country.   *T-cm*

41. Compare being in love and loving.   *T-cm*

42. Compare your life now with what it was like ten years ago.   *T-cm*

43. Compare your physical appearance now to the way you looked as a child.   *T-cm*

44. Compare two different loves.   *T-cm*

45. Compare your thoughts about the United States before you came here with your present ideas. How did you learn about the United States.   *T-cm*

46. Compare your housing now to the living quarters you had as a child.   *T-cm*

47. Compare selfishness and selflessness.   *T-cm*

48. Compare being thrifty and being cheap.   *T-cm*

49. Compare two seasons.   *T-cm*

50. Compare cats and dogs.   *T-cm*

Hopes and Fears for the Future

1. Talk about your future plans or goals.   *T-hof*

2. Tell us about what you hope for the world.   *T-hof*

3. Talk about the kind of life you hope to have.   *T-hof*

4. Talk about the things you once feared but will never fear again.   *T-hof*

5. Talk about your greatest fear for mankind.   *T-hof*

6. Talk about the hopes and fears your parents had for you.   *T-hof*

7. Talk about the hopes you once had which never came to be.   *T-hof*

8. Talk about what you hope people will do in order to live in peace.   *T-hof*

9. Talk about your hopes and dreams for your family.   *T-hof*

10. Talk about the kind of world you hope for your children.   *T-hof*

11. Tell us what you hope the world will be like twenty years from now.   *T-hof*

12. Talk about what frightens you the most about getting older.   *T-hof*

13. Talk about your fears for your family.   *T-hof*

14. Talk about what you think will happen when you die. Do you hope to find an afterlife ?   *T-hof*

15. Talk about why you look forward to the future.   *T-hof*

16. Tell us how hope changed your life.   *T-hof*

17. Tell us what changes you fear.
    T-hof

18. Talk about a great fear that you have conquered.   *T-hof*

19. Talk about an impossible dream.
    T-hof

20. Talk about a hope or dream that did come true.   *T-hof*

Personal Experiences

1. Talk about a time when you felt God was with you.   *T-per*

2. Talk about a lesson that you learned "the hard way."   *T-per*

3. Talk about one of the worst moments in your life.   *T-per*

4. Talk about somewhere that was very painful to leave.   *T-per*

5. Talk about something you did but later deeply regretted. *T-per*

6. Talk about a difficult decision that turned out to be wrong.   *T-per*

7. Talk about the time when you expected nothing and were pleasantly surprised.   *T-per*

8. Describe the greatest moment in your life.   *T-per*

9. Talk about your first true love.

10. Talk about an experience which taught you your greatest lesson about people.   *T-per*

11. Talk about a childhood experience that you will never forget.   *T-per*

12. Tell us about a frustrating experience.   *T-per*

13. Talk about a time when you were under so much pressure that you didn't think you'd survive. *T-per*

14. Tell us about a time when you found out you were wrong. *T-per*

15. Talk about an experience that completely restored your faith in the world.   *T-per*

16. Tell us about the time that you did something which embarrassed your family.   *T-per*

17. Talk about the time when you did something completely against your nature which surprised everyone you knew.   *T-per*

18. Tell us about a time when you felt a deep sense of shame. *T-per*

19. Tell us about a time when you did something completely on instinct.   *T-per*

20. Tell us about a time when you experienced a complete sense of calm and well-being.   *T-per*

21. Tell us about a time when you felt you were the center of the universe.   *T-per*

22. Talk about a time when you got caught.   *T-per*

23. Talk about a funny experience that happened to you that you will never forget.   *T-per*

24. Talk about an experience that made you aware that you weren't a child any longer.   *T-per*

25. Tell us about someone or something that has changed your life.   *T-per*

26. Talk about how your life has changed. *T-per*

27. Talk about a time when you felt life had cheated you. *T-per*

28. Talk about the problems you have had to overcome. *T-per*

29 Talk about a time when you questioned your own identity. *T-per*

30. Talk about a time when you were deeply disappointed in yourself. *T-per*

31. Talk about an incident which made you believe in fate. *T-per*

32. Talk about a time when you saw your life flashing by you. Were you frightened? *T-per*

33. Talk about a time when you were disappointed by someone or something. *T-per*

34. Tell us about someone who is dead that you really need to speak to. *T-per*

35. Talk about the time a miracle occurred in your life. *T-per*

36. Talk about a time when you lost your faith. *T-per*

Self-Description

1. Talk about what you most respect and admire in yourself. *T-sd*

2. Talk about the things you think about the most. *T-sd*

3. Talk about the things in life that mean the most to you. *T-sd*

4. Tell us about your personal weaknesses. *T-sd*

5. Tell us about what you worry about the most. *T-sd*

6. Talk about what you love about your family. *T-sd*

7. Tell us about your character strengths. *T-sd*

8. Tell us about a custom or family tradition that you have and would like to pass to your own children. *T-sd*

9. Talk about a person whom you love and could not live without. Why do you love this person so much? *T-sd*

10. Talk about the things about yourself you would like to change. *T-sd*

11. Talk about a possession you have that you could never sell. *T-sd*

12. Talk about the kind of person who would be your soulmate. *T-sd*

13. Talk about your successes in life. *T-sd*

14. Talk about what entertains you. *T-sd*

15. Talk about your favorite hideaway. *T-sd*

16. Talk about why you are the way you are. *T-sd*

17. Tell us about something or someone you really miss. *T-sd*

18. Talk about the importance of acceptance in your life. *T-sd*

19. Tell us about someone you forgave. *T-sd*

20. Talk about the importance of religion and the power of prayer in your life.   *T-sd*

21. Talk about the person you will never forgive.   *T-sd*

22. Tell us about why you gave up on someone.   *T-sd*

23. Talk about the things about life that makes you unable to ever give up.   *T-sd*

24. Talk about the person who has influenced your life the most.   *T-sd*

25. Talk about a physical trait in yourself that you wish you could change.   *T-sd*

26. Talk about the things which make you angry.   *T-sd*

27. Talk about the things you have to do but hate to do.   *T-sd*

28. Talk about your temperament and your nature.   *T-sd*

29. Tell us what it is that makes you who you are.   *T-sd*

Time Travel: The Year 2025

1. Talk about the world's greatest problems in 2025.   *T-tt*

2. Tell us about what it's like in the United States in 2025.   *T-tt*

3. Where would be the ideal place to live in 2025?   *T-tt*

4. Talk about your family and your personal changes as you imagine them to be in the year 2025.   *T-tt*

5. It's the year 2025. Talk about where you're living and what you're doing.   *T-tt*

6. The year is 2025. Tell us what changes have occurred in religion.   *T-tt*

7. Talk about family structure in the year 2025.   *T-tt*

8. Talk about the earth's population and where people are concentrated in 2025.   *T-tt*

9. Talk about the space program in 2025.   *T-tt*

10. Talk about the use of psychics and psychic traveling in the year 2025.   *T-tt*

11. Talk about all the changes in technology from now to the year 2025. Have people been able to adapt? Have basic human values changed?   *T-tt*

12. It's 2025. How is the US government different? What kind of president do we have?   *T-tt*

13. In the year 2025, what is our environment like? What animals have become extinct?   *T-tt*

14. Talk about schooling and education in 2025.   *T-tt*

15. Tell us what changes have occurred in people both physically and mentally from now until the year 2025.   *T-tt*

16. It's 2025. Talk about changes in medicine. What diseases have been cured? Are some diseases more important?   *T-tt*

17. It's 2025. Are we doing a better job of managing our planet? *T-tt*

18. In the year 2025, how long will people expect to live? How long will they be competent to work? How long will they be competent to enjoy life?   *T-tt*

19. By the year 2025, which countries will have come together to form one and which will have separated to form two or more?   *T-tt*

20. In the year 2025, what roles are men and women playing in society?   *T-tt*

Truth or Lies?

1. You are the the doctor for a woman who has been trying to become pregnant for ten years. She is 45 years old. You think the woman should accept the fact that she is infertile. What do you say to her?   *T-tl*

2. A good friend of yours has just had a nose job. You think it looks really bad and very phony. What do you say when your friend asks you what you think?   *T-tl*

3. You are pregnant and only 15 years old. You are very unhappy and feel that your parents would be extremely angry if they found out. What would you do?   *T-tl*

4. Your best friend has decided to get married. You don't like the person your friend has chosen. Do you tell your friend?   *T-tl*

5. You are 16 years old. You've just gotten your driver's license. You borrow your parents' car and accidentally hit a parked car. No one sees you. What do you do?   *T-tl*

6. You have been dating someone for two years. Last night you got drunk and had sex with your friend's best friend. Will you ever tell the person you're dating?   *T-tl*

7. Your spouse is physically abusive to you, but with five children, you have no other means of financial support. What are you going to do?   *T-tl*

8. You have gotten your girlfriend pregnant and she wants to have the baby. You feel that if she has the baby, your life is ruined. What do you do?   *T-tl*

9. Your wife has just become pregnant and the two of you are extremely happy. A good friend of yours has been trying to become pregnant for several years and has just miscarried. When you meet this friend on the street, do you tell her about your wife? *T-tl*

10. The doctor tells you your elderly parent is terminally ill and should not be excited or upset. Your parent is frightened and wants to know what the doctor said. Do you tell the truth? *T-tl*

11. Although your friend has tried to make a good impression on your parents, your parents strongly object to your friend and you think it is because your friend is of a different race. What do you say when your friend wants to know what your parents think?   *T-tl*

12. You and your spouse have been married for five years. You have been happy but lately you have begun to feel very sexually attracted to someone else. You have not acted upon this feeling but your spouse has noticed something is wrong between the two of you. Do you tell your spouse about your feelings? What do you say?   *T-tl*

13. You are a teenager and you occasionally smoke marijuana. Your parent finds a small joint in your room. What do you say it is and where do you say it came from?   *T-tl*

14. You are engaged to be married to someone you've loved for many years. Just recently you have begun to recognize that you have a sexual attraction towards someone of your own sex. What do you do?   *T-tl*

15. You are taking a test and realize that the person sitting next to you is copying from your paper. What do you do?   *T-tl*

16. Your friend bought you a birthday present that you do not like and know you would want to exchange or return. What do you say?   *T-tl*

17. You are on a first date and you are date-raped. You know your parents would never understand. What do you do?   *T-tl*

18. You are rushing out the door because you are late for an appointment. You see children throwing rocks at a window down the street. One of the children breaks it, but another is blamed. What do you do?   *T-tl*

19. Your child has never known his father because the child was conceived as the result of a rape. When your child asks, "Don't I have a dad?" what do you say?   *T-tl*

20. You are HIV positive but have been symptom free. You meet a very attractive person who wants to get to know you better. Do you tell this new admirer that you tested positive?   *T-tl*

21. You are pregnant but the father of your child has another woman and doesn't want anything more to do with you. Do you tell him about his child?   *T-tl*

22. You want to stay in this country but you do not have a green card. You need money and a friend of yours knows someone who is hiring workers without checking their immigration status. Do you apply for and take the job?   *T-tl*

23. You are homosexual but have never told your parents because you think they would never understand. What do you say when a parent asks you why you never have any dates?   *T-tl*

24. You know that many of the athletes at a competition are taking steroids. Some of these people are on your team. What do you do?   *T-tl*

25. When you and your friend leave a store at the mall, your friend shows you that she has taken something without paying for it. She seems quite proud of her accomplishment. Do you do anything?   *T-tl*

26. Without permission, you read your sister's diary and found out that she is having sex with her boyfriend. What will you do?   *T-tl*

27. While you are taking a walk, you find a wallet in the street. It contains no identification and several thousand dollars. What are you going to do?   *T-tl*

28. Your friend is quite overweight and started dieting a few months ago. Although your friend is always hungry now, you have not noticed any weight loss. What do you say when your friend asks if you notice any difference?   *T-tl*

29. Your friend has a very ugly new baby. What do you say?   *T-tl*

30. Your friend is going bald and is very sensitive about it. When he combs his hair in a different way in order to cover the bald spot, in your opinion, this only makes the spot look more noticeable. What do you say when he tells you he thinks he looks much better with this new hairstyle?   *T-tl*

31. You have just been in a fist fight with a neighborhood gang. You know if you tell anyone, the gang will come after you and your family. What do you do?   *T-tl*

GROUP CREATIVITY

These activities involve group thinking to invent a story or situation. The emphasis here is on creativity and the groups' ability to work together using many different ideas to create a mutually acceptable story line or discourse. The first activity involves pairs of students working together to invent stories to dramatize proverbs/aphorisms and superstitions for class presentation.

Procedures for Proverbs and Superstitions

Introductory Exercises

#1. As an introduction to proverbs and superstitions, have the students write several examples from their native countries with the English translation. Then the students can discuss and compare the English proverbs and superstitions, giving examples from their own countries when appropriate.

#2. Give a proverb or superstition card to a pair or small group of students. They must try to figure out the meaning and give an example. Then have the pairs or groups exchange cards. At the end of the exercise, as a class discuss the ideas brought up in the exercise.

#3. For a writing assignment, have the students compare the similarities between their proverbs (or superstitions) and those of the United States.

Creative Activities

#1. Pair up the students and have each pair choose one proverb and one superstition. Tell the students to make up a story about how the proverb or superstition came into existence. Then have the pairs present their stories to the class. The class then votes as to which pair had the most absurd (or believable) story, and that pair wins.

#2. The first step may be followed up with a writing assignment. The groups may write down their own stories. You may ask them to retell (as best they remember) one of the stories they heard from a different pair. (This can be quite funny, almost like the game of telephone but on paper.)

#3. Once the students are familiar with some of the proverbs and superstitions, put the students into small groups and give each group three cards. Each card will have a different proverb or a superstition written on it. Have each group select only one card from the three. Give the students about fifteen minutes to create a story based on the card using the superstition or proverb as the last line of their story.

Then have each group tell the story to the class. This can be done by calling on one student from a group to begin the story, and another student to continue the story, etc. until everybody in the group has participated. This can also be done having one student from a group say one line of the story, followed by the next student who would continue the story with the next line (see Chain Stories), or by simply calling on only one student from each group to tell the story.

After the groups have completed this, have the groups pass the two unused cards to another group. Again, each group has to choose a card and make up a story just as they did before. The stories will get more and more difficult as the more difficult cards come into play.

#4. You can also have the students prepare their story based on the proverb or superstition, leaving the last line out. Have the rest of the class vote on which proverb or superstition the story illustrated.

#5. Use activity #3 as the basis for a writing assignment. (See activity #2 for suggested procedures.)

#6. Alternatively, you can have the students read the writing that they did in activity #3 (making sure the last line is omitted) and have the class vote on which proverb or superstition they think the student wrote.

Proverbs

1. A bird in the hand is worth two in the bush. *GC-pr*

2. A friend in need is a friend indeed. *GC-pr*

3. A fool and his money are soon parted. *GC-pr*

4. A rolling stone gathers no moss. *GC-pr*

5. A stitch in time saves nine. *GC-pr*

6. A watched pot never boils. *GC-pr*

7. A word to the wise is sufficient. *GC-pr*

8. Absence makes the heart grow fonder. *GC-pr*

9. All that glitters is not gold. *GC-pr*

10. An apple a day keeps the doctor away. *GC-pr*

11. An ounce of prevention is worth a pound of cure. *GC-pr*

12. Beauty is as beauty does. *GC-pr*

13. Beauty is in the eye of the beholder. *GC-pr*

14. Beauty is only skin deep. *GC-pr*

15. Blood is thicker than water. *GC-pr*

16. Boys will be boys. *GC-pr*

17. Business before pleasure. *GC-pr*

18. Cash on the barrelhead. *GC-pr*

19. Cats have nine lives. *GC-pr*

20. Children should be seen and not heard. *GC-pr*

21. Cleanliness is next to godliness. *GC-pr*

22. Cowards die a thousand times before their deaths. *GC-pr*

23. Do as I say, not as I do. *GC-pr*

24. Do unto others as you would have them do unto you. *GC-pr*

25. Don't bite off more than you can chew. *GC-pr*

26. Don't bite the hand that feeds you. *GC-pr*

27. Don't burn your bridges behind you. *GC-pr*

28. Don't count your chickens before they hatch. *GC-pr*

29. Don't cry over spilled milk. *GC-pr*

30. Don't cut off your nose to spite your face. *GC-pr*

31. Don't look a gift horse in the mouth. *GC-pr*

32. Don't make a mountain out of a mole hill. *GC-pr*

33. Don't put all your eggs in one basket. *GC-pr*

34. Don't put the cart before the horse. *GC-pr*

35. Every cloud has a silver lining. *GC-pr*

36. Every dog must have its day. *GC-pr*

37. Fight fire with fire. *GC-pr*

38. Good fences make good neighbors. *GC-pr*

39. Grab the bull by the horns. *GC-pr*

40. He laughs best that laughs last. *GC-pr*

41. Haste makes waste. *GC-pr*

42. He who hesitates is lost. *GC-pr*

43. Hell hath no fury like a woman scorned. *GC-pr*

44. His bark is worse than his bite. *GC-pr*

45. Home is where the heart is. *GC-pr*

46. If at first you don't succeed, try, try again. *GC-pr*

47. If the shoe fits, wear it. *GC-pr*

48. If you can't beat 'em, join 'em. *GC-pr*

49. If you can't stand the heat, get out of the kitchen. *GC-pr*

50. If you give him an inch, he'll take a mile. *GC-pr*

51. It hurts to be beautiful. *GC-pr*

52. It's better late than never. *GC-pr*

53. It's better to be safe than sorry. *GC-pr*

54. It's better to give than to receive. *GC-pr*

55. It's better to have loved and lost than never to have loved at all. *GC-pr*

56. It's later than you think. *GC-pr*

57. It's not whether you win or lose, but how you play the game. *GC-pr*

58. It's not who you are; it's who you know. *GC-pr*

59. It's quality, not quantity, that counts. *GC-pr*

60. Judge not that you be not judged. *GC-pr*

61. Keep a stiff upper lip. *GC-pr*

62. Keep your nose out of other people's business. *GC-pr*

63. Keep your nose to the grindstone. *GC-pr*

64. Keep your wits about you. *GC-pr*

65. Laugh and the world laughs with you; cry and you cry alone. *GC-pr*

66. Lay your cards on the table. *GC-pr*

67. Leave well enough alone. *GC-pr*

68. Let sleeping dogs lie. *GC-pr*

69. Let the chips fall where they may. *GC-pr*

70. Let your conscience be your guide. *GC-pr*

71. Life is just a bowl of cherries. *GC-pr*

72. Look before you leap. *GC-pr*

73. Love is blind. *GC-pr*

74. Make hay while the sun shines. *GC-pr*

75. Necessity is the mother of invention. *GC-pr*

76. Nice guys finish last. *GC-pr*

77. No pain, no gain. *GC-pr*

78. One man's food is another man's poison. *GC-pr*

79. One picture is worth a thousand words. *GC-pr*

80. Patience is a virtue. *GC-pr*

81. People who live in glass houses shouldn't throw stones. *GC-pr*

82. Practice what you preach. *GC-pr*

83. Put your best foot forward. *GC-pr*

84. Rome wasn't built in a day. *GC-pr*

85. Silence is golden. *GC-pr*

86. Slow and steady wins the race. *GC-pr*

87. Some people have all the luck. *GC-pr*

88. Spare the rod, spoil the child. *GC-pr*

83. Speak softly and carry a big stick. *GC-pr*

89. The grass is always greener on the other side. *GC-pr*

90. The higher they climb, the farther they fall.

91. The only thing we have to fear is fear itself. *GC-pr*

92. The squeaky wheel always gets the grease. *GC-pr*

93. The way to a man's heart is through his stomach. *GC-pr*

94. There are plenty of fish in the sea. *GC-pr*

95. There's more than one way to skin a cat. *GC-pr*

96. There's more to it than meets the eye. *GC-pr*

97. There's no time like the present. *GC-pr*

98. Time and tide wait for no man. *GC-pr*

99. Time is money. *GC-pr*

100. Too many cooks spoil the broth. *GC-pr*

101. Two wrongs don't make a right. *GC-pr*

102. Turn about is fair play. *GC-pr*

103. Variety is the spice of life. *GC-pr*

104. Virtue is its own rewrd. *GC-pr*

105. Waste not, want not. *GC-pr*

106. What goes around comes around. *GC-pr*

107. What goes up, must come down. *GC-pr*

108. What's good for the goose is good for the gander. *GC-pr*

109. When in Rome, do as the Romans do. *GC-pr*

110. When it rains, it pours. *GC-pr*

111. When the cat's away, the mice will play. *GC-pr*

112. When the going gets tough, the tough get going. *GC-pr*

113. Where there's smoke, there's fire. *GC-pr*

105. You can attract more bees with honey than you can with vinegar. *GC-pr*

106. You can't burn a candle at both ends. *GC-pr*

107. You can't change a leopard's spots. *GC-pr*

108. You can't fight city hall. *GC-pr*

109. You can't have your cake and eat it too. *GC-pr*

110. You can't teach an old dog new tricks. *GC-pr*

111. You can't tell a book by its cover. *GC-pr*

112. You get what you pay for. *GC-pr*

113. You're never too old to learn. *GC-pr*

Superstitions

1. Finding a four leaf clover is good luck. *GP-Su*

2. The number seven is lucky. *GP-Su*

3. A rabbit's food is lucky. *GP-Su*

4. A horseshoe is lucky. *GP-Su*

5. If you say something is good, knock on wood to retain the good luck. *GP-Su*

6. Finding a penny heads up is lucky. *GP-Su*

7. If you make a wish on a falling star or the first star you see at night, it will come true. *GP-Su*

8. If you throw a coin into a pool of water and make a wish, it will come true. *GP-Su*

9. If your nose itches, you should kiss a fool. *GP-Su*

10. If your ears are burning, someone is talking about you. *GP-Su*

11. Accidents happen in threes. *GP-Su*

12. A widow's peak is a sign of beauty. *GP-Su*

13. Cross your fingers when lying, to avoid bad luck. *GP-Su*

14. If you cross your fingers, your wish may come true. *GP-Su*

15. Avoid walking under a ladder because it's bad luck. *GP-Su*

16. Spilling salt is bad luck; throw some over your right shoulder to get some luck back. *GP-Su*

17. An open umbrella in the house is unlucky. *GP-Su*

18. It's bad luck when a black cat crosses your path. *GP-Su*

19. Anything that has the number 13 is unlucky, especially Friday the 13th. *GP-Su*

20. If you use a match to light three cigarettes, it is unlucky. *GP-Su*

21. Stepping on cracks will break your mother's back. *GP-Su*

22. A mirror face down is bad luck. *GP-Su*

23. The Queen of Spades is the card of death. *GP-Su*

24. If you break a mirror you will have seven years of bad luck. *GP-Su*

25. If your tooth falls out, place it under your pillow at night and the tooth fairy will exchange if for something valuable. *GP-Su*

Group Creativity: Chain Stories

The class invents a story, using a chain story card as the opening line. This activity stimulates creative thinking and expression.

Procedures for Chain Stories

#1. Divide the students into two or three groups. Give one student in each group a card. This student will read it and then make up a sentence to follow logically in the story. The next student continues the story with another sentence and so forth. End the story by calling "time" after three to five minutes. Have the groups pass their card to another group and start the procedure again.

#2. The students, working in pairs or individually, can make up a story using the card as the first sentence. These stories can be presented to the class.

#3. Use procedure 1 or 2 but also give a secret word to each group, pair or individual student. At some time during the story, the student or group must use that word. After the story is completed, listening students must guess what the others' secret words were.

#4. The students can write their own stories. This can be done under the pressure of a time limitation to encourage spontaneity, or it can be done without a time limit to work on accuracy of expression. You may or may not want to give the students words to include in their stories.

Chain Stories

1. One day I decided to take a bus as far as it went.   *GC-cs*

2. One day I decided to go somewhere so no one could find me.   *GC-cs*

3. One day I woke up late.   *GC-cs*

4. One day I forgot where I was supposed to be.   *GC-cs*

5. One day I saw a very attractive person at a bus stop.   *GC-cs*

6. One day I was walking on some very slippery ice.   *GC-cs*

7. One day I decided to take a short cut through the park.   *GC-cs*

8. One day I was taking a walk and saw some smoke.   *GC-cs*

9. One day I had a big fight with my best friend.   *GC-cs*

10. One day I woke up and thought it was Sunday.   *GC-cs*

11. One day I decided to do something totally out of character.   *GC-cs*

12. One day I decided to visit someone I hadn't seen in a long, long time.   *GC-cs*

13. One day I decided to take a trip somewhere.   *GC-cs*

14. One day I wanted to do something unique.   *GC-cs*

15. One day I decided to dress up as somebody else.   *GC-cs*

16. One day I decided to buy something that was alive.   *GC-cs*

17. One day I decided not to be honest with anyone for the whole day.   *GC-cs*

18. One day I decided to show the world how I really felt.   *GC-cs*

19. One day I decided to take a chance.   *GC-cs*

20. One day I decided to be aggressive.   *GC-cs*

21. One day I decided to make some trouble.   *GC-cs*

22. One morning I woke up and realized I was alive.   *GC-cs*

23. One night I decided to go exploring.   *GC-cs*

24. One day I was riding in my car and found that I had no brakes.   *GC-cs*

25. One day I was taking a walk when I heard a scream.   *GC-cs*

26. One day I opened my front door. I looked down, and at my feet I saw a tiny baby smiling up at me.   *GC-cs*

27. One day I decided to visit a prison.   *GC-cs*

28. One day I was riding my bike when I saw a fantastic sight.   *GC-cs*

29. One day I woke up and realized I was in love.   *GC-cs*

30. One day I just started walking.   *GC-cs*

31. One day I just felt like screaming the whole day.   *GC-cs*

32. One day I realized I was alone in this world.   *GC-cs*

33. One day I wanted to do all the things that I had always been afraid of doing.   *GC-cs*

34. One day I wanted to tell everybody the truth about what I thought of them.   *GC-cs*

35. One day I ran out of gas in the middle of nowhere.   *GC-cs*

36. One day I decided to run away.   *GC-cs*

37. One day I was walking along and it started to rain.   *GC-cs*

38. One evening I heard a strange noise.   *GC-cs*

39. One day I thought I saw a ghost.   *GC-cs*

40. One day I decided to play a joke on someone with no sense of humor.   *GC-cs*

41. One night I was awakened in the middle of the night by an alien being.   *GC-cs*

42. One day I decided to change my life.   *GC-cs*

43. One day I decided to quit my job.   *GC-cs*

44. One day I decided to get a body part pierced.   *GC-cs*

45. One day I ran into someone I had thought was dead.   *GC-cs*

46. One day I decided to be really bad.   *GC-cs*

47. One day I decided to eat everything I wanted without worrying about calories.   *GC-cs*

48. One day I decided to clean out the garage.   *GC-cs*

49. One afternoon I saw a very attractive hitchhiker at the side of the road.   *GC-cs*

50. One day I decided to stop and talk to a homeless person. *GC-cs*

51. One day I decided to act my age.   *GC-cs*

52. One day I decided to destroy something.   *GC-cs*

53. One day I decided to do what I've always wanted.   *GC-cs*

54. One day I put on a mask. *GC-cs*

55. One day I decided to befriend every person I met.   *GC-cs*

56. One day I lost my voice.   *GC-cs*

57. One day I really felt close to my cat.   *GC-cs*

58. One day I felt the floor below me fall away.   *GC-cs*

59. One day I woke up in another century.   *GC-cs*

60. One day I decided to get a tattoo.   *GC-cs*

61. One day in a strange city, I saw a woman in a black trench coat. A fire engine turned the corner behind me. I felt somehow that I'd been there before.   *GC-cs*

62. One night I just couldn't fall asleep.   *GC-cs*

Group Creativity: Find Out

The students are challenged to invent conversations through which they can cleverly find out specific information without letting on what they are trying to learn. This activity stimulates creative thinking and expression.

Procedures for Find Out

#1. Divide the students into two groups and divide the topic cards equally between them. Have the students decide collectively on how to elicit the response or action requested on each card without directly asking. You may give the students thirty minutes to work on five or six cards.

Choose a card from one group (Group A, for example). Give the card to one of the students from that group (Group A), and ask that student to come up to the front of the class. Ask that student (from Group A) to choose a person from another group (Group B) to be a partner. The student from Group A must now try to make conversation to elicit the requested information from the partner (from Group B).

Additionally, when the conversation is completed, the partner (from Group B) must not know what the other student (from Group A) was trying to elicit. In other words, the partner (from Group B) should not be able to guess what was written on the card.

#2. As a follow-up or homework assignment, the students can write a dialogue based on the cards used in class, or if you prefer, different *Find Out* cards.

Find Out

1. Find out if your partner had a dream last night. *GC-fo*

2. Find out the nationality of your partner's parents. *GC-fo*

3. Find out if your partner sleeps with or without pajamas. *GC-fo*

4. Find out what day of the week your partner was born. *GC-fo*

5. Find out the name of your partner's childhood sweetheart. *GC-fo*

6. Find out if your partner has a lucky number. *GC-fo*

7. Find out if your partner wears a hairpiece. *GC-fo*

8. Find out if your partner is pregnant. *GC-fo*

9. Find out how many traffic accidents your partner has had. *GC-fo*

10. Find out how old your partner was when your partner learned about sex. *GC-fo*

11. Find out if your partner has ever lost money gamblig. *GC-fo*

12. Find out your partner's favorite foreign food. *GC-fo*

13. Find out how much money your partner spends a month. *GC-fo*

14. Find out your partner's favorite song. *GC-fo*

15. Find out if your partner ever wears a hat. *GC-fo*

16. Find out if your partner took a shower or a bath this morning. *GC-fo*

17. Find out how long your partner takes in the bathroom in the morning. *GC-fo*

18. Find out your partner's shoe size. *GC-fo*

19. Find out the name of your partner's first grade teacher. *GC-fo*

20. Find out if your partner has any bad habits. *GC-fo*

Group Creativity:
Get Your Partner

A student is challenged to invent a clever way to get another student to do some specific thing without being asked directly to do it. This activity stimulates creative thinking and expression.

Procedures for Get Your Partner

#1. Follow the procedure in the first paragraph for *Find Out*.

Explain to the students that you have an action or activity of some sort written on the card. Have the student who has the card (from Group A, for example) try to get a partner (from Group B) to do the activity without asking directly.

This time, at the end of the activity the partner (from Group B) should be able to easily guess what action the student with the card (from Group A) was trying to evoke.

You may want to limit the time to only a few minutes for each pair.

#2. For homework, give the students new *Get Your Partner* cards and have them come prepared to use them in the next class. Tell the students that they will have only one minute in class to "get their partners".

Get Your Partner

1. Get your partner to whistle.
   GC-gyp

2. Get your partner to take off your shoe.
   GC-gyp

3. Get your partner to stick out her tongue.
   GC-gyp

4. Get your partner to make a funny face.
   GC-gyp

5. Get your partner to take out the trash.
   GC-gyp

6. Get your partner to offer to make you dinner.
   GC-gyp

7. Get your partner to clean the room.
   GC-gyp

8. Get your partner to scratch his head.
   GC-gyp

9. Get your partner to bend over.
   GC-gyp

10. Get your partner to take off an article of clothing.
    GC-gyp

11. Get your partner to sing.
    GC-gyp

12. Get your partner to imitate someone.
    GC-gyp

13. Get your partner to imitate an animal sound.
    GC-gyp

14. Get your partner to hit himself.
    GC-gyp

15. Get your partner to scratch your back.
    GC-gyp

16. Get your partner to hold your hand.
    GC-gyp

17. Get your partner to laugh loudly.
    GC-gyp

18. Get your partner to raise both hands over her head.
    GC-gyp

19. Get your partner to turn around 360 degrees.
    GC-gyp

20. Get your partner to jump.
    GC-gyp

21. Get your partner to draw a cow and a bull.
    GC-gyp

22. Get your partner to cough and then yawn.
    GC-gyp

23. Get your partner to tell a lie.
    GC-gyp

24. Get your partner to give you his phone number.
    GC-gyp

25. Get your partner to pick up a chair.
    GC-gyp

26. Get your partner to tell a funny story.
    GC-gyp

DISCUSSIONS

These topics are generally controversial and they lend themselves to discussion and debate, requiring the student to think about and express opinions on important issues in a group situation.

Procedures for Discussions

#1. Choose a topic card. Introduce and explain the topic so that all the students understand the meanings and implications. Go over some of the vocabulary associated with the topic. Ask each student to make an opening statement about the topic and then lead a discussion based on the opening statements, asking for clarification, elaboration, and agreement/disagreement.

#2. Divide the students into two or three large groups. Then have the students sit in a circle and place their mistake cards on a table near them. Assign a topic card and a leader to each group. The leader reads the card to the group and makes sure all the students in the group speak. As the group is sharing ideas, circulate to the different groups and spot-record the mistakes heard. At the end of the discussion, the groups can exchange topics and once again discuss while you monitor each group. At the end of the specified time, the students look at their mistake cards and correct the errors.

#3. After introducing the topic, ask the class how many people agree with the card, and how many don't. The students can be divided into two groups which must prepare arguments either supporting or disputing the topic. Then have the groups debate the issue, or have only one or two representatives from the two groups discuss the topic. You may or may not wish to monitor mistakes.

#4. Divide the class into two groups, the students who agree with the card and the students who disagree. Put one student who agrees in a pair with a student who disagrees. Then time the pairs for ten minutes and have them discuss the issue. At the end of the time, ask students individually if they have changed their attitudes after talking to their partners.

#5. The students can be asked to write their ideas about the topic, either before the discussion, as an introduction, or after the class discussion as a follow-up.

Opinions

1. Women belong at home taking care of children. *D-op*

2. In these times, it is better not to have any children. *D-op*

3. People are animals and, therefore, are not monogamous by nature. *D-op*

4. If your parents were alcoholic, chances are you will become an alcoholic too. *D-op*

5. Men and women are emotionally different. *D-op*

6. Teachers should not socialize with students. *D-op*

7. Life in the United States is much too easy. *D-op*

8. Spanking and hitting children is a form of child abuse. *D-op*

9. Children nowadays have no respect for themselves, their parents or anyone else. *D-op*

10. People in the United States are very friendly. *D-op*

11. It is important for both spouses to be virgins when they marry. *D-op*

12. Living together before marriage should be required, like getting a driving permit before you get the license. *D-op*

13. Everyone should keep a gun in the home for self-protection. *D-op*

14. Sex offenders should be castrated. *D-op*

15. All children who deliberately commit crimes should be tried as adults. *D-op*

16. It is dangerous these days to send a child to public school. *D-op*

17. Watching a lot of TV and rock videos can make people violent. *D-op*

18. If you want to exercise you must join a gym or health club. *D-op*

19. Foreign cars are better than American cars. *D-op*

20. Classical music is superior to popular music. *D-op*

21. Women who get raped usually deserve it. *D-op*

22. Americans drink too much. *D-op*

23. Americans and Europeans focus too much on physical beauty. *D-op*

24. Americans are fat because they eat too much junk food. *D-op*

25. Children get a better education outside the classroom. *D-op*

26. There should be no homework given in schools. *D-op*

27. The Test of English as a Foreign Language should not be required for admission to a United States university. *D-op*

28. English should be the only international language. *D-op*

29. Homosexual couples should be allowed to adopt children. *D-op*

30. People should not marry outside their religion. *D-op*

31. Interracial marriages should be encouraged. *D-op*

32. Adopted children should always be able to find out who their natural parents are. *D-op*

33. Everyone should have a pet. *D-op*

34. Parents should be stricter with their children. *D-op*

35. Rock and roll will never die. *D-op*

36. People over 40 should not have children. *D-op*

37. Women are naturally better care givers. *D-op*

38. We should get rid of the Academy Awards and give awards to regular people who are doing exceptional jobs. *D-op*

39. Watching TV wastes time. *D-op*

40. People should never work in the same office or department as their spouses. *D-op*

41. There should be no seniority at work. The people who work best should be promoted first. *D-op*

42. No one needs to see a psychiatrist or psychologist if they have friends to talk with. *D-op*

43. Sunbathing in the nude should not be illegal. *D-op*

44. If your religion forbids it, your children should not have to have inoculations in order to attend school. *D-op*

45. The US should give amnesty to all illegal immigrants. *D-op*

46. Newspapers have a responsibility to report all the facts, no matter who may be hurt. *D-op*

47. Immigration into the United States should be free and unlimited. *D-op*

48. If a child commits a crime, both the parent of the child and the child should be put in jail. *D-op*

49. There can be absolutely no defense for children who kill their parents. *D-op*

50. So many terrible things happened to the American Indians that it is no wonder they are all alcoholics. *D-op*

51. Buying "mail order brides" is like purchasing a baby and should be illegal. *D-op*

52. Everyone should go to college. *D-op*

53. The Catholic Church should not permit people to annul their marriages. *D-op*

54. The speed limit needs to be raised. *D-op*

55. Orphanages are not as good as foster homes. *D-op*

Philosophical Issues

1. There is no God. *D-ph*

2. People are basically good. *D-ph*

3. All governments are corrupt. *D-ph*

4. War is inevitable. *D-ph*

5. There is no such thing as fate. *D-ph*

6. All religions are the same. *D-ph*

7. People are the same everywhere. *D-ph*

8. People who are terminally ill should be allowed to die if they or their families so choose. *D-ph*

9. Suicide should not be considered a crime. *D-ph*

10. There isn't enough joy in the world. *D-ph*

11. Life is a miracle from God. D-ph

12. People made up religions to comfort themselves.   D-ph

13. Religion rarely brings people together. Usually it drives groups of people apart.   D-ph

14. There can be no happiness without money.   D-ph

15. There is no such thing as love.   D-ph

16. The difficulties we face make us better people.   D-ph

17. Cheating is a fact of life.   D-ph

18. Life gets worse the older you get.   D-ph

19. What you do in life is what you get from it.   D-ph

20. Honor and integrity mean nothing anymore.   D-ph

21. There is nothing worse in life than death.   D-ph

22. Violence can never be justified.   D-ph

23. It is in man's nature to fight, hunt, and destroy others. D-ph

24. If women were in charge of all the governments, there would be no war.   D-ph

25. Having children is a birthright which should never be denied to anyone by anyone else.   D-ph

26. Art is not as important as politics.   D-ph

27. Everyone has and needs some form of vice.   D-ph

28. We should disobey a law that is contrary to our own beliefs. D-ph

29. There is no justification for terrorism.   D-ph

30. You cannot make anyone else happy. Being happy is up to the individual.   D-ph

31. Experience is more important than schooling.   D-ph

32. The sexes are not and should not be equal.   D-ph

33. If people felt more shame, we would live in a better society.   D-ph

34. Power and money can bring anyone happiness.   D-ph

Social Issues

1. Television is more harmful than it is beneficial for society. D-soc

2. Abortion is a form of legalized murder.   D-soc

3. Prostitution should be legalized.   D-soc

4. Cigarette smoking must be banned entirely and the sale of tobacco made illegal.   D-soc

5. Birth control is against God's will.   D-soc

6. People with HIV and AIDS should be required to wear something warning people of their condition.   D-soc

7. Today the real education children get in school is training in violence which they see, talk about, and live with every day.   D-soc

8. Capital punishment is a deterrent against crime. *D-soc*

9. The government should supply free housing for everyone. *D-soc*

10. No one should be allowed to have billions of dollars while other people have nothing. *D-soc*

11. The drinking age needs to be lowered, because prohibiting teens just leads to more drinking. *D-soc*

12. Our society is falling apart. *D-soc*

13. Drunk drivers should receive mandatory jail sentences. *D-soc*

14. Illegal drug laws should be made much stronger and enforced. Addicts need to be taken off the streets and away from our children. *D-soc*

15. Homosexuality is genetic. It is not a choice and can never be changed. *D-soc*

16. AIDS is on this earth to annihilate homosexuality. *D-soc*

17. Our society is slowly deteriorating because of too much leniency. *D-soc*

18. More emphasis should be placed on individuality rather than fitting into society. *D-soc*

19. Neighbors need to be informed when an ex-convict is living in their area. *D-soc*

20. Women will never be equal to men in the eyes of men. *D-soc*

21. Most convalescent and nursing homes are ill-equipped and poorly staffed. It is actually more dangerous for aging people to live in such a home than to live by themselves. *D-soc*

22. All pornographic material should be censored. *D-soc*

23. Medical care should be free for all people. *D-soc*

24. You really cannot trust anybody. *D-soc*

25. When people who are on government assistance have more children, the government should cut off their benefits. *D-soc*

26. Population control should be strictly enforced by the government. *D-soc*

27. The law protects the criminals and puts the victims on trial. *D-soc*

28. Protecting the environment and endangered species should not be a priority now. *D-soc*

29. Professional sports teams should be operated by governments, not private enterprise. *D-soc*

30. Pornographic theaters and shops should never be allowed in residential neighborhoods. *D-soc*

31. Since safe disposal of nuclear waste is impossible, we must find other energy alternatives. *D-soc*

32. The government should immediately enforce tough anti-pollution laws. *D-soc*

33. People who develop drug and alcohol problems should have their children taken away from them. *D-soc*

34. Slavery still exists in the form of marriage. *D-soc*

35. There is no such thing as "love". *D-soc*

World Issues

1. We can and must put a stop to world hunger. *D-wld*

2. Countries need to ban together and enact laws prohibiting border dumping. *D-wld*

3. There should be one and only one international language. *D-wld*

4. Traffic laws should be standardized in all countries of the world. *D-wld*

5. Peace will never be attained throughout the world because countries are greedy and want more power. *D-wld*

6. The UN is just another name for the US. *D-wld*

7. In some ways, third world countries are more developed than "developed" countries. *D-wld*

8. The US takes advantage of smaller, weaker nations in order to exploit them economically. *D-wld*

9. The US gives too much financial assistance to developing countries when the money should be used for the US. *D-wld*

10. The space program will move more rapidly if countries individually work to send only their astronauts into space, because competition among nations produces better results. *D-wld*

11. Scientists from all countries need to work together trying to find cures for widespread and incurable diseases. *D-wld*

12. One country cannot save another. Even if a country asks for intervention, other countries ought to focus on their own problems and mind their own business. *D-wld*

13. There should be no extradition of international terrorists. *D-wld*

14. All governments should extend aid to any country torn apart by a natural disaster. *D-wld*

15. Diplomats should not have any kind of diplomatic immunity. *D-wld*

16. The war on drugs will never be won on an international level. It must be won locally. *D-wld*

17. Countries should not trust other countries. We need to always have spies to find out other countries' secrets. *D-wld*

18. There is no way to find abducted children on an international level. *D-wld*

19. All countries should totally disarm in the interest of world peace. *D-wld*

20. We must find ways to preserve our planet. It is dying. *D-wld*

POSTSCRIPT

The topics presented in this book are merely tools to stimulate thought and expression. The activities presented can be used to practice not only how to speak, but how to respond appropriately in different situations. During this process, the teacher and students can identify incorrect speech and work on improving language skills.

The number of topics one could make up is endless. It is the author's hope that students, as well as their teachers, will be encouraged to use or discard the topics presented in this book depending on the interests of the class and also to make up additional topics of particular interest to the students. And yet, actually, the topics themselves are irrelevant; what is important is real, stimulating conversation. That is what we hope this book will facilitate. If the students want to change a topic or speak about something else that seems significant to them, we encourage the teacher to be flexible enough to accept this change and respect any attempt at verbal communication that is meaningful to the student.

It is in this atmosphere of mutual respect between teacher and student, and between student and student, that ideas can be shared, cultures and traditions opened to view, and human beings understood by other human beings. After all, what other purpose is there to communication?

- N.E.Z.

Conversation Strategies: Pair and Group Activities for Developing Communicative Competence by David Kehe and Peggy Dustin Kehe with illustrations by Andrew Toos. A student text with 24 activities giving practice with the words, phrases and conventions used to maintain effective control of conversations. Strategies include polite forms, correction, agreement and disagreement, summarization, clarifications, follow-up questions, interruptions, and avoiding conversation killers.

Cue Cards: Nations of the World by Raymond C. Clark and Anna Mussman. A Set of 42 *Cue Cards* with detailed information about the most populous nations of the world. Photocopyable masters.

Cue Cards: Famous Women of the 20th Century by Lisa F. DeWitt. A collection of *Cue Cards* featuring 40 bio-sketches of women from 18 countries who have shaped or are shaping the world we live in. Photocopyable masters.

Index Card Games for ESL, edited by Raymond C. Clark. 6 game techniques for developing vocabulary, sentence/paragraph structure, pronunciation and spelling, questioning, and conversation skills through student-centered conversation activities. A "starter kit" of sample games at the elementary, intermediate and advanced levels is given after each explanation. Also available in French and Spanish.

More Index Card Games and Activities for English. 9 new language learning games using 3x5 index cards. The focus of these activities is on conversation skill building. The format includes explanations of the game techniques and a "starter kit" of sample games at various proficiency levels. The samples may be photocopied.

Lexicarry by Patrick R. Moran. Students develop vocabulary using the active method, discussing drawings that illustrate the functional language used in ritual situations (greetings, condolence, invitations), sequences of actions (lose, look for, find), related actions (walk, run, skip, march), vocabulary topics (tools, color, clothing, sounds), operations (changing a light bulb), and such places as the office, living room, airport, and street corner.

Operations in English: 55 Natural and Logical Sequences for Language Acquisition by Gayle Nelson and Thomas Winters. Often humorous classroom activities in which students working in pairs communicate naturally and accurately to accomplish set tasks step by step.

The World: The 1990's from the Pages of a Real Small-town Daily Newspaper, edited by John N. Miller and Raymond C. Clark. 288 articles offer a wide-ranging selection of conversation topics from human interest stories to international sports and economics and science. Discussion topics are suggested for each article. There is a topical index. 6 teaching techniques are explained for use with any news article.

Resources for Developing Conversation Skills, concluded

Story Cards: North American Indian Tales, compiled by Susannah J. Clark and illustrated in color by Ken Rainbow Cougar Edwards. Students choose one of the 48 illustrated *Story Cards,* read the story and then tell it from memory to a partner or to the class. Each story can be the basis for fascinating intercultural discussions.

Story Cards: Aesop's Fables, compiled by Raymond C. Clark, illustrated in color by Hannah Bonner. 48 of Aesop's wonderful, classic stories, some well known and others not so familiar, can be used as the basis for many different conversation activities.

Story Cards: The Tales of Nasreddin Hodja, compiled by Raymond C. Clark, illustrated by Robert MacLean. These 40 stories about a funny and wise old Turk have been told and embellished by adults and children over the whole world touched by Islam for over 700 years. The cards can be used for practicing story telling and as the basis for many conversations on human nature and cultural comparisons.

Cultural Awareness Teaching Techniques by Jan Gaston. 20 conversation activities designed to help students develop cultural awareness and sensitivity. They can be used in any multi-cultural language classroom and in other training and orientation programs with students of at least intermediate language ability.

Related materials

Writing Inspirations: A Fundex of Individualized Writing Activities for English Language Practice, by Arlene Marcus. 170 writing-topic activity cards, containing hundreds of writing tasks ready to be photocopied and mounted on 8x5 index cards for students to choose from.

The ESL Miscellany by Raymond C. Clark, Patrick R. Moran, and Arthur A. Burrows. A compendium of information and vocabulary lists that will be the inspiration for many cultural- and language-related conversations as well as many teacher-created lessons. Fully photocopyable.

Discovery Trail by Mark Feder. 900 questions (90 in each of 10 areas - grammar, proverbs, idioms, geography and history, US citizenship, etc.) are the basis for a board game or a quiz card game, either of which will stimulate hours of fun and varied conversation and language learning.

Families: 10 Card Games for Language Learners, by Marjorie S. Fuchs, Jane Critchley, and Thomas Pyle. Students enjoy conversation, question and answer practice, and vocabulary building in any language using 40 humorous, full-color cards – 10 families each with a mother, father, daughter, and son. Each card has 8 features to ask about: clothes, hat, shoes, expression/emotions, object, money (numbers), transportation, and time.

All of the above materials are available from **Pro Lingua Associates**, *15 Elm Street, Btrattleboro, Vermont 05301 USA* ✧ *800 366 4775*